CELEBRATE
with BABS

CELEBRATE
with BABS

HOLIDAY RECIPES & FAMILY TRADITIONS

BARBARA COSTELLO

Publisher Mike Sanders
Art & Design Director William Thomas
Senior Editor Alexandra Andrzejewski
Senior Designer Rebecca Batchelor

First American Edition, 2022
Published in the United States by DK Publishing
6081 E. 82nd Street, Indianapolis, IN 46250

Published in the United States
by Dorling Kindersley Limited.

Library of Congress Catalog Number: 2021944179
ISBN: 978-0-7440-5692-1

DK books are available at special discounts when
purchased in bulk for sales promotions, premiums,
fundraising, or educational use. For details, contact:
SpecialSales@dk.com

Printed and bound in Canada

For the curious
www.dk.com

FOR

Mary, my spiritual Mother,

Minnie, my mother,

Vincenza, my grandmother,

Hazel, my mother-in-love, and

Ida, my surrogate mother—

because you can never have too many mothers!

CONTENTS

NEW YEAR'S DAY *festivities*..............20

SUPER BOWL *bash*...................36

VALENTINE'S DAY *dinner*.................50

ST. PATRICK'S DAY *celebrations*......66

EASTER *luncheon*......................80

MOTHER'S DAY *brunch*.........................98

BIRTHDAY CAKE *bash*.........................114

SUMMER *barbecue*..................................124

OKTOBERFEST *party*..........................146

HALLOWEEN *festivities*......................160

THANKSGIVING *feast*.........................178

CHRISTMAS EVE *festival*...................202

CHRISTMAS DAY *celebrations*........222

INDEX...............................246

BEYOND BRUNCH

This all started with a simple, wooden recipe box. In that box are generations of precious recipes, compiled over a half century and served at holiday celebrations throughout the years. These recipes evoke crystal-clear memories of days long past, celebrating holidays with family and friends, many of whom are no longer here.

The food-centered celebrations and traditions passed down to me have shaped who I am today. I grew up in a large Italian and Lebanese family, and although I only have one older sister, I always felt I came from a family of many siblings. When we gathered for holidays or Sunday dinners at Grandma and Grandpa's, the house was overflowing with my 20 aunts and uncles, 16 first cousins, and most importantly an abundance of love. There were so many people in the family that even after my husband Bill and I were married, we still had to sit at the designated kids' table.

In those days, food was the center of any family gathering (as it is now, but even more so back then). My grandmother and mom, along with my aunts, would begin preparing for a holiday sometimes weeks in advance. Each had a role to play. What I remember most was the energy of the celebrations they curated—the din of multiple conversations going on at once, the laughter, the time spent with my cousins, and especially the abundance and many courses of food; just when you thought it had to be it, something else emerged from the kitchen. It was sheer *abbondanza* on all levels.

Many years ago, we moved far from my family. So much of that family has now passed, but they remain with me because of the holiday traditions they've handed down. Those early impressions truly never left me. The torch of holiday celebrations has been passed to me and my husband, and now to our own children. They've been tweaked and changed to now become our traditions. Yet, the thread holding together all these celebrations throughout the years, first and foremost, has always been the food.

Preparing certain dishes once per year at a certain time of year is like a rhythm that celebrates the dance of life. Life is a celebration, and the traditions found in these celebrations bring the richness of family, friends, and food together. These celebrations connect us to each other, to our roots. Those connections will hopefully be passed on to our four children and eight grandchildren when we are no longer here.

This book holds the holiday recipes and traditions that have been part of my life, passed down through generations of family and friends. I hope you enjoy them, and the stories as well. It's never too late to begin your own traditions, which will long be remembered...because now is the time to celebrate this great gift of life! No matter what your family makeup is, no matter who you celebrate with, no matter who passes you the salt when it's most necessary, it is never too late to start your own story.

Xoxo,
Babs

THE ART OF CELEBRATING

I have a host of tips to alleviate some of the stresses of entertaining, from making the choice to throw a celebration, to prepping the food, to cleaning up afterward. I think the most important thing to remember is that it's really all about relationships and the warmth and love of opening your heart and home to the most important people in your life. The memories and traditions will flow from that in a truly authentic way.

I hope you not only enjoy the delicious dishes in this book (ones I have been preparing for my own family for so long), but more importantly, I also want to inspire you to welcome others to your table. Open your home to someone you may not have thought to open it to in the past. I want to gift you the confidence to host anything from a big holiday like Thanksgiving, to a small Fourth of July summer barbecue with friends. Any opportunity to open your heart and home and to spread warmth and hospitality through food is the glue that, for me, holds all of these traditions together. I am passing down to you what I've held so near and dear to my heart over the last 50 years. Now it's your turn to carry the torch!

THE PARTY

Ready to host that party, or not so sure? It's an honor to bring people together, so find a reason to celebrate, make some family and friends feel special by inviting them to your home, and dive into the world of entertaining.

YOU WON'T REGRET THE CHOICE TO ENTERTAIN

Sometimes people shy away from entertaining. Let's face it, people are busy with their routine schedules, and time is precious. Sometimes the most difficult thing is to just make a commitment and not look back. If you second guess yourself about that, you'll come up with 110 reasons why now is not a good time to host a special holiday for family and friends. You know that once that commitment is made, it's full steam ahead with planning, cooking, cleaning, decorating, and more.

You will never regret the choice to bring the special people in your life together, welcoming them warmly into your home for a celebration. The memories and traditions you will be creating through this labor of love are priceless—not just for you, but for your loved ones and generations to come.

WHAT ARE WE CELEBRATING?

Well, the obvious is all the religious and cultural holidays on our calendar. However, reasons to celebrate life are everywhere, like celebrating the change of seasons, a new baby, a baptism, a graduation, Oktoberfest, Derby Day...you get the idea. There are endless reasons to celebrate this gift of life.

MAKING IT SPECIAL FOR EVERYONE

Try to get the family involved in the party. You are planting the seeds in their lives so that in the future, they will have the confidence to carry on family traditions they have observed and in which they have participated. The silver lining is that the more they feel part of the planning process, the more they will help and support you—a win-win!

Remember the whole point of entertaining is to make memories and build your own family traditions. My advice is to treat family like company and company like family. If you relax and remember that, then when guests arrive, they will immediately sense your welcoming warmth. You will be well on your way to hosting a memory-making party.

THE INVITE LIST

If planning a family event, your guest list is most likely set. However, if you are hosting a party for friends, you should be mindful of the chemistry of the guests you are inviting and how they will gel as a group. This is especially important if you are hosting a sit-down dinner.

MAKING IT HAPPEN

Now the point is not to feel frazzled and exhausted by the time the doorbell rings. You want to get everything done—and I mean everything done—ahead of time. Get your grocery shopping done as early as possible so there are no loose ends; several days ahead is good. Decorate and set the table a few days before the party. All your food prepping should be done the day before with most dishes assembled and even some cooked.

THE PARTY SPACE

Keep in mind the size of your entertaining space. Do you have adequate room to invite all the friends you would like to include? Enough table space? Chairs? Perhaps a buffet would be the way to go, depending on logistics and the vibe you want to convey. All this has to be considered before sending out those invites.

A SPECIAL TABLE SETTING

Don't be afraid to use your best dishes and flatware. Your wedding china and sterling silver that you never use? Well, now is the time to use it. What are you saving it for? Also, don't worry if you don't have anything extra special—it's the connecting with others that counts the most.

If you want to "properly" set a formal table, just remember you're going from left to right, with the napkin, salad fork, and dinner fork to the left of the plate; and to the right of the plate is the knife with blade facing the plate and soup spoon or teaspoon, if using. Glasses are on the right just above the knife and spoon, with wine on the outside and water on the inside in a diagonal line.

If you are hosting a sit-down dinner, you might want to consider place cards. We don't use these for family events, but it might be a nice touch when hosting friends to arrange a seating plan that considers the chemistry between people. You are trying to promote lively conversation and a fun atmosphere at the table.

If you are having a buffet, it's a good idea to use individual trays for your guests if they are not being seated at a table. I have a great set of wicker trays that I bought at the Christmas Tree Shop for $1 each! Remember to have small salt and pepper shakers at both ends of the dining table or on the buffet table.

You don't have to splurge on flowers for the table. Sometimes small bud vases on the table make more of a statement than some huge, pricey centerpiece. Candles are always lovely on the table and throughout your entertaining space. Again, small votive candles might be just enough.

THE FOOD

As you will see, most of the recipes in this book of celebrations can be easily made ahead, and some must absolutely be made ahead—by the day of the party, you can focus on completing last minute touches and not having a nervous breakdown in the kitchen!

MENU PLANNING

There are a few factors to consider once you decide on a menu. The first is this: not everything has to be homemade! If baking is not your thing and throws you for a loop, then visit a wonderful local bakery and give them some business. Once desserts and bread are covered, then you can focus on the basics of the menu.

FOOD PREP: DO IT!

Do not try to prepare all of your dishes the day of the festivity. Before the big day arrives, the most important thing you can do is to have all of the dishes either already cooked or prepped as much as you possibly can. Assemble all ingredients, every last one, including that ¼ teaspoon of salt. Prepare each ingredient according to the recipe so it's ready to toss in and move on. If you need half of a large onion chopped, it's time to chop that onion.

Set it aside and proceed to the next ingredient. It's also a good idea to use a baking sheet and assemble all the ingredients for a particular dish you are making, keeping everything together and organized. Plus, you can easily double-check all ingredients, making sure everything is ready for the cooking process. You could even prep several dishes at once. Just make sure you have several baking sheets separating the ingredients for the individual recipes, and don't forget to include a copy of the recipe on the tray.

TIMING YOUR FOOD

Remember to consider if dishes must rest or chill before serving, and plan accordingly. An oven schedule is super important. Be strategic and know exactly what's getting cooked when and for how long. Make sure this is posted in a prominent place. In fact, I like to use the inside of my kitchen cabinets as recipe organizers. I just print up the recipe and tape it to the inside cabinet with everything right at my fingertips, including the oven schedule.

You are all ready to start cooking! Wasn't that easy?

BABS SAYS...

"When people are RSVP'ing and offering to bring something, take advantage of that! When we have holiday family parties, people are actually assigned certain dishes or beverages and ice."

PARTY DAY

You made it! Planning is half of the fun, but the real prize is the energizing din of family and friends making connections and memories in the space you've worked so hard to create.

THE ATMOSPHERE

Don't forget to turn on all the lights throughout the house, and leave them on a dim setting. It's also a nice touch to have a pot of potpourri simmering on the stove as your guests arrive. When they enter your home, the mood has been set. Is the music queued up to softly play when the party begins?

BABS SAYS...

"Don't forget about you! Make sure you schedule enough time to relax and get dressed, ready to enjoy your own party. After everything you have done to make this celebration happen, you deserve to look and feel your best."

Lowering the temperature before the guests arrive is a good idea, since depending on the number of people attending, the house can become overheated in no time.

BEVERAGES

The day of the party, plan on setting up a self-serve beverage station away from the kitchen. Guests will eventually end up in the kitchen, but when they first arrive and you would like to have some peace in the kitchen, it's a good idea to have this station all set and ready to go.

Don't forget the ice! Both an ice bucket for the drinks, as well as a large cooler filled with ice. Store party beverages in the cooler to free up much needed refrigerator space.

BABS SAYS...

"Don't forget to spruce up the bathroom! Your guests will enjoy lovely, festive hand towels, scented soap, and a little bud vase with fresh flowers. Check the toilet paper situation and make sure you have a full roll. That's the last thing you want to worry about when you have a house full of guests!"

Sometimes it's nice to offer a signature drink that is unique for the holiday. You'll find lots of those in this book! It's also a nice touch to offer coffee and tea after dinner. Get the coffee pot ready to go so you only have to plug it in and press "brew." If you have an espresso machine, offer that as well. You can even set up an after-dinner self-serve beverage station where all these selections are offered with cups, saucers, cream, sugar, and spoons all set out. If using paper cups, pick up a festive, good-quality selection.

Assign someone the job of filling the water glasses with ice and water (whether tap, bottled, or bubbly) before dinner is served. Uncorking wine and letting the bottles breathe should be done ahead of time so it's all ready to pour.

APPETIZERS

If the appetizer doesn't need to be heated, set it out throughout the entertaining space. However, be mindful of what foods are going to be served at the main meal so as not to overload on the appetizers. For holidays like Thanksgiving or Christmas, just a simple cheese, fruit, and cracker platter and small bowls of nuts may be enough.

BABS SAYS...

"An important tip is to make sure the dishwasher is empty and the sink is clear of dishes before guests arrive. When the table is cleared before dessert, the dishes can go right in."

TRADITIONS & ENTERTAINMENT

We do like to play games when having family over for the holidays. We even include the little ones and have had a great time playing charades. For Christmas, we distribute printouts of some of our favorite Christmas carols and sing around the tree. Sometimes for an icebreaker, we pin a famous or historical figure's name on the back of each guest as they arrive, and as they mingle, they have to guess who they are by asking each other yes or no questions.

My grandkids have always been involved in the big day. The young ones spend some time upon arrival coloring place mats for the family table. I always have an arts and crafts table set up for this fun activity, also giving their parents a little break. The kids also always lead us in grace before we begin the meal.

A fun thing we have done for many years at the Thanksgiving table is to place two dried beans at each place setting. Once we are all seated and grace has been said, a small cup is passed from person to person, and as one bean is dropped in the cup, the person announces something or someone they are thankful for. The cup is passed around twice. The raw beans are then used in making a special soup from the turkey carcass, Gratitude Soup.

These are just a few examples of traditions we can't imagine our holidays without, but there are so many sweet rituals you can introduce now and bring back year after year. Check out the section "Traditions to Make Your Own" in each chapter for some ideas to get started.

Remember, these are just some ideas and not meant to overwhelm. The goal is to throw not the perfect party, but rather a memorable one with the people you love.

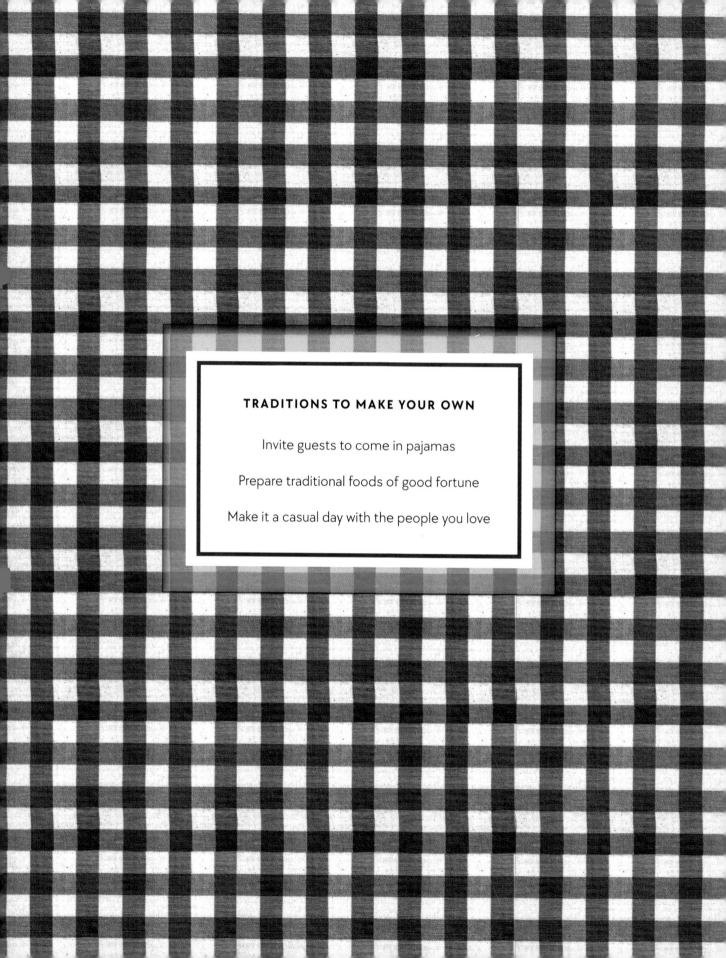

TRADITIONS TO MAKE YOUR OWN

Invite guests to come in pajamas

Prepare traditional foods of good fortune

Make it a casual day with the people you love

NEW YEAR'S DAY
festivities

One of my earliest entertaining memories was the first time I hosted a family holiday almost 50 years ago. My husband and I were finally granted the responsibility of overseeing New Year's Day. We had just bought our first home in La Grange Park, Illinois, so the older generation thought, "let's give the kids a chance at entertaining now that they have a space to host the family." Since everyone was up late on New Year's Eve, our first New Year's Day party came with two rules. It had to start later in the afternoon so all could sleep in, and it had to be casual...no fancy sit-down meal. A leisurely buffet and pj's encouraged a tradition we continue to this day.

No matter what the year—1972 or 2022—you'll always find football on the TV, someone in the family arguing about who cheated during our intense annual family card game, and most importantly, a beautiful spread of food with fortune and good luck at the forefront of the menu.

Everything on the menu was easily prepared in advance. The brisket was the centerpiece of the meal. It was prepped the night before and went into a low-temperature oven hours before the party began. By the time the family arrived, the house was filled with the aroma of a smoky barbecue. The cheeseball was also made a few days before the party. All I needed to do was roll it in the chopped pecans, and the appetizer was ready to go. A do-it-yourself Bloody Mary bar was another convenience at this causal holiday celebration.

Side dishes have changed over time. However, for many years now, we have maintained the southern tradition of eating black-eyed peas, greens, and pork on New Year's Day, as these are foods believed to bring good fortune in the new year ahead. The extra tasty four-layer cake, a family favorite, was a succulent dessert ready when we were.

For us, New Year's Day is the official close of the holiday "food feast" that begins on Thanksgiving Day each year. New Year's Day was and always is a time to relax, kick back with family, and give thanks for the year past and the year ahead. Cheers!

ON THE
TABLE

Cheddar Pecan Cheeseball. 24

Good Luck Salad 27

Virginia au Gratin Potatoes 29

Oven-Barbecued Brisket 31

Mom's Four-Layer Delight 33

Bloody Marys 35

CHEDDAR PECAN CHEESEBALL

I have been making this cheeseball for at least 40 years and have brought it to more get-togethers and family celebrations than I can count. What's great about this recipe is that it serves a crowd, it's easy to make, and most importantly, it's absolutely delicious. When made ahead, the flavors of this savory appetizer actually taste better. A holiday at our house wouldn't be the same without this on the table. This is a colorful appetizer that can be enjoyed throughout the holiday season or even at a family barbecue—it's that versatile.

prep time
10 minutes, plus
at least 1 hour to chill

cook time
none

serves
12

INGREDIENTS

2 (8 oz/225g) pkgs cream cheese, softened

2 cups shredded sharp cheddar cheese

1 tbsp finely chopped pimiento

1 tbsp finely chopped green pepper

1 tbsp finely chopped yellow onion

2 tsp Worcestershire sauce

1 tsp fresh lemon juice

Dash of cayenne

Dash of salt

Coarsely crushed raw pecans, to cover

Crackers, to serve

DIRECTIONS

1. In a large bowl, stir together the cream cheese and shredded cheddar until well blended. Stir in the pimiento, green pepper, onion, Worcestershire sauce, lemon juice, cayenne, and salt until well combined.

2. Refrigerate, covered, for about 1 hour, or until chilled. Shape into a ball, and roll in the pecan pieces. Serve immediately with crackers.

MAKE IT AHEAD
Make this up to 2 days in advance, and store, covered, in the refrigerator. It tastes best when you make it ahead of time, and that adds to the convenience of this tried-and-true recipe! Roll it in coarsely crushed pecans right before serving.

GOOD LUCK SALAD
(KALE & SPINACH SALAD WITH BLACK-EYED PEAS)

prep time
20 minutes

cook time
none

serves
8

One of the traditions for bringing prosperity to the new year is eating certain foods on New Year's Day. Our family has always followed the tradition of eating black-eyed peas and pork on this holiday. Some traditions mention black-eyed peas and greens, so we covered all bases with this delicious salad topped with crumbled bacon. Happy, healthy, and prosperous New Year to you!

MAKE IT AHEAD
You can prepare all of the ingredients 1 day ahead of time, but wait to dress the salad until serving.

INGREDIENTS

1 bunch curly kale, ribbing discarded, cut into thick ribbons

8 oz (225g) baby spinach

1 small red onion, thinly sliced

1 medium red or yellow bell pepper, diced

¾ cup cooked or canned black-eyed peas, drained and rinsed

4 slices bacon, cooked and crumbled

2 tbsp chopped chives (optional), to garnish

Dressing:

½ cup extra-virgin olive oil

½ cup balsamic vinegar

1 tbsp lemon juice

½ tsp garlic powder

½ tsp salt

¼ tsp freshly ground black pepper

DIRECTIONS

1. Prepare the dressing. In a small bowl, whisk together all ingredients until emulsified.

2. In a large serving bowl, add the kale, spinach, onion, bell pepper, black-eyed peas, and crumbled bacon.

3. Toss with the desired amount of dressing. Top with chives (if using), and serve.

VIRGINIA AU GRATIN POTATOES

prep time
30 minutes

cook time
2 hours

serves
10–12

When we moved to Virginia, we didn't know a soul, but the first weekend in our new neighborhood, we were invited to a progressive dinner—a party where the adults would eat appetizers together at someone's home, then split into smaller groups to enjoy dinner at another host's house and then reconvene for coffee and dessert. It's a ton of fun and really encourages neighbors to bond. These potatoes were served at my very first progressive dinner, and I had to have the recipe. If you're looking for the perfect cheesy, creamy au gratin potatoes, look no further.

INGREDIENTS

6 medium russet potatoes, peeled and thinly sliced

¼ cup all-purpose flour, divided

¾ tsp kosher salt, divided

¼ cup unsalted butter, softened, divided

3 cups whole milk

2 cups shredded cheddar cheese

DIRECTIONS

1. Preheat the oven to 350°F (180°C). Grease a 9 x 13-inch (23 x 33cm) baking dish.

2. Arrange a single, overlapping layer of the thinly sliced potatoes in the dish. Sprinkle the layer of potatoes with 2 tablespoons flour and ¼ tsp salt. Dot with 2 tablespoons softened butter. Repeat to make a second layer. For the third layer, use the remainder of the potatoes and the remaining ¼ teaspoon salt.

3. Pour the milk evenly over the potatoes. Sprinkle the shredded cheddar cheese evenly over the top. Cover tightly with foil. Bake for 2 hours, or until browned and the potatoes are tender, removing the foil during the last 45 minutes. Serve immediately.

BABS SAYS...

Shredding the cheese yourself gives you the best melt and flavor.

I use a mandoline to slice the potatoes. If you don't have a mandoline and the potato is wobbly on your surface, slice off a thin piece along the length of the potato, then turn the potato cut-side down so it sits on the flat side for easier slicing.

MAKE IT AHEAD

Precook for 1 hour and 15 minutes up to 2 days in advance. Before serving, finish cooking, uncovered, for the last 45 minutes.

You can also freeze the casserole up to 3 months before serving. Cook for 1 hour and 45 minutes, and let cool. Cover tightly with plastic wrap and then foil. Thaw completely in the refrigerator before reheating, uncovered.

OVEN-BARBECUED BRISKET

If you want something that's easily prepped the night before, popped into the oven and slow-cooked for hours while you go about your day—and is beyond delicious!—this checks all the boxes. This succulent meat just falls apart and tastes like it's been slowly cooked in a smoker somewhere in the heart of Texas. This is one of my family's all-time favorite entrées and will be your family's, as well. It's such an easy dish to prepare after all the holiday festivities wind down and as a new year begins. Kick back and turn on the games because dinner is cooking.

prep time
10 minutes, plus overnight to marinate

cook time
5 hours

serves
8–10

BABS SAYS...
Slice against the grain! Just look for the lines on the meat, and slice the opposite way.

Leftovers make for great sandwiches the next day.

INGREDIENTS

4–5 lb (2–2.25kg) beef brisket

½ tsp onion salt

½ tsp celery salt

½ tsp garlic powder

2 tbsp liquid smoke

¼ cup + 2 tbsp Worcestershire sauce

¾ cup barbecue sauce, such as Sweet Baby Ray's Original

DIRECTIONS

1. Sprinkle the beef with the onion salt, celery salt, and garlic powder. Place it in a shallow baking dish. Pour liquid smoke and Worcestershire sauce over the meat, and cover with heavy foil, sealing tightly. Refrigerate overnight.

2. Preheat the oven to 300°F (150°C). Bake, covered, for 4 to 4 ½ hours, or until tender.

3. Pour the barbecue sauce over the beef, and bake, uncovered, for an additional 30 minutes.

4. Slice the meat against the grain, and serve immediately, drizzled with juices from the pan (if desired). Store leftovers in an airtight container in the refrigerator for up to 5 days or in the freezer for up to 3 months.

MOM'S FOUR-LAYER DELIGHT

prep time
30 minutes, plus
at least 4 hours
to chill

cook time
15 minutes

serves
12

My mom was an amazing baker. Her go-to cookies and cakes were loved by all, but she also loved to try new recipes. This was one of her favorite "new" desserts that she first made for my son Shawn's christening. To this day, I remember how everyone went wild for it. It was one of her most-requested desserts, brought to many, many family parties thereafter. The cool, creamy layers sit on a butter and nut crust—the perfect contrast. My mom used chocolate pudding for the pudding layer, but experimenting with different pudding choices is always fun!

INGREDIENTS

Chocolate shavings, to top

First layer:

1 cup (128g) all-purpose flour

½ cup (112g) unsalted butter, melted

½ cup (60g) chopped raw pecans

Second layer:

1 cup (115g) sifted powdered sugar

8 oz (225g) full-fat cream cheese, softened

4 oz (110g) Cool Whip

Third layer:

2 (3.4 oz/96g) boxes instant chocolate pudding

3 cups whole milk

1 tsp pure vanilla extract

Fourth layer:

8 oz (225g) full-fat cream cheese, softened

1 cup (115g) sifted powdered sugar

2 cups heavy whipping cream

1 tbsp pure vanilla extract

DIRECTIONS

1. Preheat the oven to 350°F (180°C). For the first layer, in a small bowl, combine the flour, butter, and pecans. Press the mixture evenly into the bottom of a 9 x 13-inch (23 x 33cm) baking dish. Bake for 15 minutes, or until lightly browned. Cool completely.

2. For the second layer, in the bowl of a stand mixer fitted with the paddle attachment, cream together the powdered sugar and cream cheese on medium-high speed. Fold in the Cool Whip. Spread the mixture evenly over the cooled crust.

3. For the third layer, in a medium bowl, mix together the instant chocolate pudding, milk, and vanilla until well combined. When the pudding starts to set, spread it evenly over the cream cheese layer.

4. For the fourth layer, in the bowl of the stand mixer fitted with the paddle attachment, beat the cream cheese and powdered sugar on medium speed for 1 minute, or until stiff peaks form. Transfer to another bowl and set aside. To the bowl of the stand mixer, add the heavy whipping cream and vanilla. Beat on high speed until soft peaks form. Add in the cream cheese mixture, and beat on medium speed until creamy, 1 to 2 minutes. Spread evenly over the top of the pudding layer.

5. Top with chocolate shavings. Cover and refrigerate for at least 4 hours, or until well chilled. Slice and serve. Store leftovers tightly covered in the refrigerator for up to 4 days.

BABS SAYS...

For the fourth layer, instead of the heavy cream recipe, you can substitute the other half of the Cool Whip container (4 oz/110g), which is what my mom always used to do.

MAKE IT AHEAD

You can fully prepare this dessert up to 4 days in advance.

BLOODY MARYS

For our family, the drink of choice on New Year's Day has always been and will always be the Bloody Mary. It really fits with our New Year's Day theme of relaxing with family as dinner cooks low and slow. The best part about my New Year's Day Bloody Mary is the garnish bar where everyone assembles their perfect glass. For a make-ahead option that takes my classic Bloody Mary up a notch, try my daughter Erin's Bloody Mary Mix.

prep time
15 minutes

cook time
none

serves
8–10

INGREDIENTS

2½ cups good vodka
3¾ cups tomato juice
1¼ cups fresh lemon juice
10 dashes Tabasco sauce
10 dashes Worcestershire sauce
1 tbsp prepared horseradish
1 tbsp balsamic vinegar
1 tsp fine sea salt
1 tsp freshly ground black pepper
1 tsp celery seed

Garnishes:
Bacon slices
Celery sticks
Cheddar cheese cubes
Cocktail onions
Cucumber spears
Shrimp
Jalapeño slices
Lemon wedges
Lime wedges
Olives

Rim:
5 tbsp kosher salt
1 tbsp ground celery seed
1 tbsp lemon pepper
1 tbsp sweet paprika
Lime wedges

DIRECTIONS

1. Pour all of the ingredients into a large pitcher or bowl, and stir to combine. For extra fun, set up a complete garnish station with skewers.

2. For the rim mixture, mix all of the seasonings together and store in a small container. When ready to use, pour some on a small plate. Moisten the rim with a lime wedge, and dip into the seasoning mixture.

3. Fill a tall glass with lots of ice and then add the tomato mixture. Go to town with your favorite garnishes!

BABS SAYS...

Having a self-serve beverage bar takes some pressure off of the host.

If you want to kick your Bloody Mary up a bit try:

Erin's Bloody Mary Mix
1 garlic clove
½ avocado
1 (46 fl oz/1.36L) can tomato juice
1 tsp prepared horseradish
1½ tsp hot sauce
1½ tsp celery salt
3 tbsp lemon juice
2 tsp A.1. Sauce
¼ cup Worcestershire sauce
2 tsp freshly cracked black pepper
2 fl oz (60ml) tequila or vodka per drink

In a food processor or blender, purée the garlic clove, avocado, and 2 cups tomato juice until smooth. Add the blended mixture to a lidded glass bottle, and stir in the remaining ingredients except the tequila or vodka. Refrigerate. Add the tequila or vodka to each glass, top with the mix, stir, garnish, and enjoy!

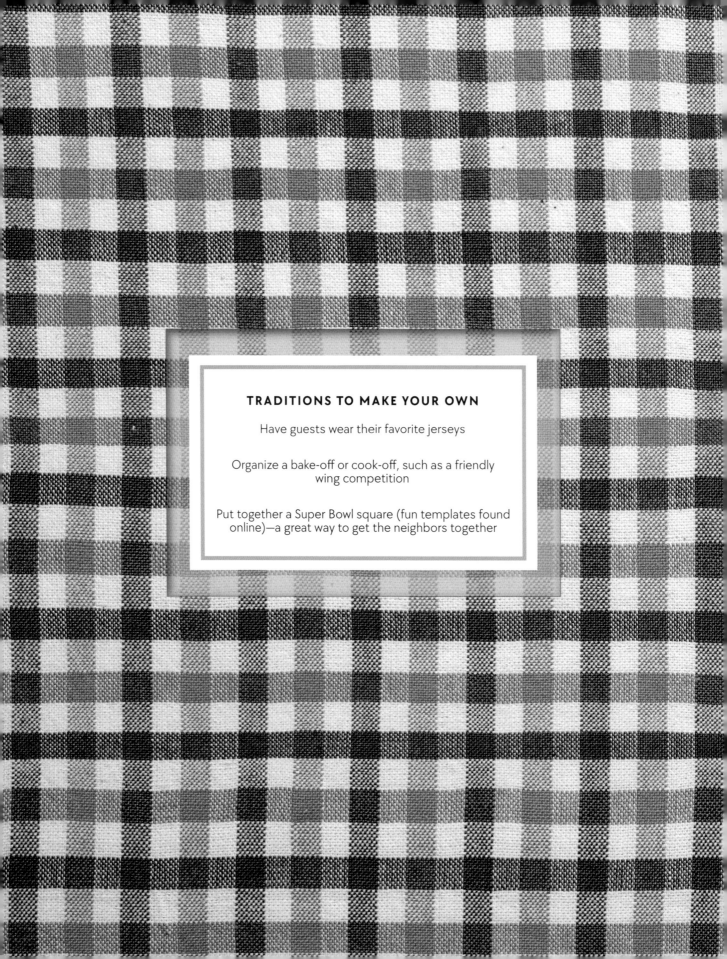

TRADITIONS TO MAKE YOUR OWN

Have guests wear their favorite jerseys

Organize a bake-off or cook-off, such as a friendly
wing competition

Put together a Super Bowl square (fun templates found
online)—a great way to get the neighbors together

SUPER BOWL
bash

My Super Bowl experience began many years ago. I traveled from Chicago to Miami with my lifelong friend and college roommate, Sandy. We had gone down to Florida to stay with family friends of hers over our semester break. The morning of Super Bowl Sunday, Sandy and I went out for breakfast and decided on the spur of the moment, "we should head over to the Orange Bowl to see if we can get some last minute tickets." We took our paper place mats, turned them over, and in large letters wrote, **NEED TICKETS.** For $20 each, Sandy and I found ourselves at one of the most famous Super Bowls: Joe Namath and the New York Jets vs. Johnny Unitas and the Baltimore Colts...the rest is Super Bowl history.

Years later, I still celebrate the Super Bowl, but in a vastly different way. For us, everything about this iconic Sunday is social, including the food. Whether at a party (we always made it a point to leave at halftime to spend the rest of the game with our kids) or celebrating at home, there's nothing like a Super Bowl Sunday spread. A buffet works best where the food is available when hunger strikes. People will graze depending on what's going on in the big game. It's also about friendly competition and placing your wager in the pool. This invites people who aren't so much into the game to be attentive in hope of their square being a big winner.

Being from Chicago, all of us are serious Bears fans. Back in 1986, when our baby Elizabeth was only a few months old, the Bears were in it. Even though our team has so far only made it to the big game twice, we still look forward to it year after year. Remember the Super Bowl Shuffle? Well, we knew every word because our kids played that video incessantly.

Now that our kids are grown with little ones of their own, memories of even the smallest celebrations hold a large place in my heart. Nothing is too small to turn into a tradition, and celebrating Super Bowl Sunday is one of ours.

ON THE
TABLE

Hot Corn Dip. 41

Bobby's Court Buffalo Wings. . .42

Slow-Cooked Pulled Pork
Sandwiches with Pickled
Red Onions. 45

Sausage Bisquick Bites 47

Texas Sheet Cake 49

HOT CORN DIP

prep time
10 minutes

cook time
35 minutes

serves
10–12

The Super Bowl is a big deal in our family. We're from the windy, broad-shouldered city of Chicago and serious sports fans. We're also very serious about our dips, and this is one of the best corn dips you will ever taste. It balances just the right amount of spiciness with the coolness of the creamy cheeses. Serve with crackers, tortilla chips, or veggies, and it's a winner every time.

INGREDIENTS

1½ cups shredded pepper jack cheese, divided

8 oz (225g) cream cheese, softened

½ cup sour cream

2 (15 oz/420g) cans sweet yellow and white corn, drained (see Babs Says…)

1 (10 oz/285g) can Ro-Tel with Green Chilies, drained

½ tsp smoked paprika

½ tsp granulated garlic

½ tsp sea salt

¼ tsp chili powder

¼ tsp ground cumin

Crackers, tortilla chips, or veggies, to serve

DIRECTIONS

1. Preheat the oven to 350°F (180°C). Grease an 8 x 8-inch (20 x 20cm) or 2-quart (2L) square casserole dish.

2. In a large bowl, add 1 cup pepper jack, the cream cheese, sour cream, corn, Ro-Tel, paprika, garlic, salt, chili powder, and cumin. Stir to thoroughly combine. Transfer the mixture to the prepared dish. Top evenly with the remaining ½ cup pepper jack.

3. Bake for 30 to 35 minutes, or until hot and bubbly. Serve immediately with an assortment of crackers, tortilla chips, and veggies.

BABS SAYS…
If you can't find the mixed corn, use a can of yellow and a can of white corn. You can also use Green Giant canned Mexicorn.

MAKE IT AHEAD
Fully prepare this up to 5 days ahead of time. Store unbaked and tightly covered in the refrigerator. Bring it to room temperature and bake as instructed.

BOBBY'S COURT BUFFALO WINGS

After our move from Virginia, we settled in Ridgefield, Connecticut, and settled in a great neighborhood on Bobby's Court, filled with families with lots of kids. The neighbors planned many get-togethers throughout the year. One of the families hailed from Buffalo (birthplace of the buffalo wing) and served their rendition during the neighborhood Super Bowl party. I will never make wings any other way. Just don't forget the celery sticks and blue cheese dressing. Our love for these wings has now been passed down to my grandson Matthew. These are his absolute favorite—he even takes them cold to the golf course.

prep time
20 minutes

cook time
1 hour 15 minutes

serves
4

INGREDIENTS

3 lbs (1.5kg) fresh whole chicken wings

1 cup all-purpose flour

Cayenne, to taste

½ tsp salt

½ tsp freshly ground black pepper

Celery sticks and blue cheese dressing, to serve

Basting Sauce:

½ cup ketchup

¼ cup salted butter, melted

1 (0.7 oz/19g) pkg Good Seasons Italian Salad Dressing Mix

¼ cup firmly packed brown sugar

1 tsp celery salt

1½ tsp ground ginger

½ cup water

2–4 tbsp Frank's RedHot Sauce (adjust according to heat preference)

DIRECTIONS

1. Cover a large baking sheet with foil and spray with olive oil. Preheat the oven to 400°F (200°C). Prepare the basting sauce. In a medium bowl, combine all of the ingredients. Set aside.

2. With a sharp knife, divide the chicken wings at the joints, setting aside the bony piece for another use, such as chicken stock.

3. In a gallon-sized resealable bag, add the flour, cayenne, salt, and pepper. Shake to combine. Working in batches, add the chicken wing drums and flats, and shake to thoroughly coat with the mixture. Evenly arrange the floured wings on the prepared sheet.

4. Bake for 45 minutes, turning once halfway through. Remove the wings from the oven, and immediately baste each wing with the sauce. Return the wings to the oven, and bake for an additional 10 minutes. Repeat the basting process a total of 3 times, turning the wings each time and baking for 10 minutes.

5. Serve immediately with celery sticks and blue cheese dressing.

MAKE IT AHEAD
Fully bake the wings up to 2 days in advance, refrigerating in an airtight container. Bring them to room temperature and reheat in the oven at 350°F (180°C) for 5 to 6 minutes. Turn them over, and continue reheating for another 5 to 6 minutes. They also may be frozen for up to 1 month in an airtight container; thaw before reheating.

SLOW-COOKED PULLED PORK SANDWICHES
WITH PICKLED RED ONIONS

prep time

10 minutes, plus up to 3 days to marinate, plus preparing pickled red onions (if desired)

cook time

11 hours

serves

10–12

This is the easiest and closest recipe I use to re-create that slow-smoked pulled pork classic, and it's become a Super Bowl staple enjoyed by all in our family. This tender, moist, barbecued pulled pork is as easy as massaging a rub on the meat and popping it into your slow cooker. It feeds a crowd, and if you decide to top the pork with the pickled onions and add a side of coleslaw, it scores a touchdown every time.

INGREDIENTS

6–8 lb (2.75–4kg) bone-in pork shoulder roast

¾ tsp liquid smoke

¼ cup apple juice

1 cup barbecue sauce, such as Sweet Baby Ray's Original, plus more to serve

Brioche buns, to serve

Pickled red onions, to serve

Dry Rub:

1 tbsp freshly ground black pepper

1 tsp cayenne

2 tbsp chili powder

2 tbsp ground cumin

2 tbsp dark brown sugar

1 tbsp dried oregano

4 tbsp sweet paprika

2 tbsp kosher salt

1 tbsp granulated sugar

1 tbsp ground white pepper

DIRECTIONS

1. Prepare the dry rub. In a medium bowl, stir together all of the rub seasonings. Massage the rub into all parts of the pork roast. Wrap the seasoned roast tightly in 2 layers of plastic wrap, and refrigerate for at least 3 hours or up to 3 days. (The longer it rests, the better.)

2. Unwrap the roast. Place it in a slow cooker. Add the liquid smoke and apple juice. Cook on low for 8 to 10 hours, or until tender and falling off the bone.

3. Transfer the roast to a cutting board, and shred the meat. Discard the fat and bone.

4. Place the shredded meat back into the slow cooker. Toss with the barbecue sauce. Cook on low for 30 to 60 minutes, or until hot.

5. Prepare sandwiches on brioche buns with additional barbecue sauce. Top with pickled red onions.

PICKLED RED ONIONS

1 medium red onion

1 clove garlic (whole)

½ cup water

¼ cup red wine vinegar

¼ cup apple cider vinegar

1 tbsp pure maple syrup

1 bay leaf

½ tsp salt

½ tsp whole peppercorns

Dash of red pepper flakes

1. With a mandoline, thinly slice the onion. To a pint-sized canning jar, add the onion slices and the whole garlic clove.

2. In a small saucepan, bring the water, red wine vinegar, apple cider vinegar, maple syrup, bay leaf, salt, peppercorns, and red pepper flakes to a boil over medium heat. Once boiling, remove from the heat and pour the mixture over the onions. Make sure to press down the onions so all are covered with the pickling mixture. Let cool to room temperature, or about 30 minutes.

3. Once cooled, refrigerate overnight before serving. This makes about 2 cups onions. Store tightly sealed in the refrigerator for up to 1 month. These really add a punch to the slow-cooked pulled pork sandwiches, as well as salads, tacos, nachos, sandwiches, and more.

SAUSAGE BISQUICK BITES

prep time
15 minutes

cook time
20 minutes

yield
36

When we moved to Richmond, Virginia, we settled in a wonderful planned community called Brandermill, buying a house in the Winterberry Ridge neighborhood. It was a perfect mix of transplanted northerners and native southerners. Since this was a new community, there was lots of socializing with progressive dinners, Super Bowl parties, and intimate get-togethers. One appetizer that was standard, no matter what the event, were these favorite four-ingredient sausage bites.

INGREDIENTS

3 scant cups Original Bisquick

1 lb (450g) uncooked spicy breakfast sausage, such as Jimmy Dean or Bob Evans

½ cup whole milk

1 lb (450g) sharp cheddar cheese, freshly grated (see Babs Says...)

Sauce for dipping, such as honey mustard

DIRECTIONS

1. Preheat the oven to 350°F (180°C). Line 1 or 2 baking sheets with parchment paper. In a stand mixer fitted with the paddle attachment, add all of the ingredients and mix on medium speed until well combined.

2. Using a 1½-inch (3.75cm) cookie scoop, form the mixture into balls.

3. Arrange the balls on the prepared baking sheets 1 to 2 inches apart. Bake for 20 minutes, or until golden brown. Serve immediately with your favorite dipping sauce—mine is honey mustard!

BABS SAYS...

Grating your own cheese makes for a moist sausage ball. You can get creative with what cheese you use, but sharp cheddar is our favorite.

Feel free to mix in some chopped, fresh onion and herbs of your choice. I like to add ¼ to ½ teaspoon cayenne for an extra kick.

MAKE IT AHEAD

These can be prepared 1 day in advance and refrigerated in an airtight container until ready to cook. Uncooked sausage balls can also be frozen in a freezer-safe bag for up to 4 months—freeze them in an even layer on a baking sheet until solid, and then transfer to the bag. To bake, let thaw for 20 minutes, then bake as directed.

TEXAS SHEET CAKE

This is the ultimate chocolate sheet cake—it serves a crowd. It's really a cross between a cake and a brownie. So if that's not enough, how about pouring warm chocolate icing over the hot cake as it comes out of the oven? Is your mouth watering yet? No wonder this cake is one of our all-time family favorite desserts. Everything is bigger in Texas, so this cake has truly been appropriately named. It's a big, delicious, chocolatey delight!

prep time
30 minutes, plus 30 minutes to set

cook time
30 minutes

serves
24

INGREDIENTS

Batter:

2 cups (256g) all-purpose flour

2 cups (400g) granulated sugar

1 cup (224g) unsalted butter

1 cup water

¼ cup (28g) cocoa powder

½ cup buttermilk

1 tsp baking soda

½ tsp ground cinnamon

½ tsp salt

2 large eggs, slightly beaten

1 tsp pure vanilla extract

Frosting:

½ cup (112g) unsalted butter

¼ cup (28g) cocoa powder

5 tbsp whole milk

1 tsp pure vanilla extract

1 lb (450g) powdered sugar

½ cup (57g) chopped raw walnuts (optional)

DIRECTIONS

1. Preheat the oven to 400°F (200°C). Grease an 11 x 16-inch (28 x 41cm) rimmed sheet pan. Make the batter. Sift the flour and sugar into a large bowl.

2. To a small saucepan, add the butter, water, and cocoa powder. Bring to a rapid boil, and then pour over the flour mixture. Whisk well.

3. Add the buttermilk, baking soda, cinnamon, salt, slightly beaten eggs, and vanilla to the flour-butter mixture. Whisk well. Pour the batter into the prepared pan. Bake for 20 minutes, or until a toothpick inserted in the center comes out clean.

4. About 5 minutes before the cake is finished baking, make the frosting. In the same small saucepan, bring the butter, cocoa powder, and milk to a boil. Remove from the heat. Whisk in the vanilla and powdered sugar until thoroughly combined.

5. While the cake is still very warm, pour the frosting in an even layer over the cake. Top with the walnuts (if using) before the frosting sets. Let stand for 30 minutes. Cut into about 24 squares, and serve. Store leftovers tightly covered at room temperature.

MAKE IT AHEAD

Prepare up to 5 days in advance. Store tightly covered at room temperature. The fully baked, frosted, and cooled cake can also be frozen in the sheet pan. Wrap tightly in plastic wrap, and then wrap in foil. Freeze for up to 6 months. When ready to eat, remove from the freezer, unwrap, and let it come to room temperature.

TRADITIONS TO MAKE YOUR OWN

Create a cozy, candlelit meal at home
for two or more

Write a little note of love and encouragement, and
place at each table setting

Teach your loved ones about the history
of holidays and traditions

VALENTINE'S DAY
dinner

When we were young, my husband, Bill, would make reservations at a lovely restaurant for Valentine's Day. That ended when we realized the regular menus were not available and the prices had doubled. We decided sharing a delicious dinner at home could be just as special. This began our annual Valentine's Day dinner, a beautiful meal that started with two and which grew with the addition of each child.

Valentine's Day has always been a day set aside to remind your loved ones that they are special and cherished. One thing that I've always done as a mom is to teach my children the history and traditions of holidays. Valentine's Day is no different. Tradition tells us it all started with a Roman nobleman named Valentine. He had converted to a new religion and was caught officiating at the wedding of a Roman soldier and his bride. The soldier and bride were arrested, but since Valentine was an aristocrat, he was simply issued a stern warning. While the two were imprisoned, Valentine would send them verbal messages of encouragement through the jail keeper's daughter, along with little torn paper hearts. That gesture of love and friendship has now evolved into a holiday celebrated every February 14th, Valentine's Day. Those torn paper hearts given centuries ago are now homemade cards or elaborate store-bought ones, gifts of chocolate and candy, and special shared dinners.

From my days teaching preschool to 3- and 4-year-olds, my days as a wife, and my days as both a mom and a grandmother, what I've learned most is that it does not matter if you are 3 or 93—everyone could use some words of encouragement, endearment, and love. If Valentine's Day teaches us anything, it's that words and actions matter. To me, Valentine's Day is a day to show our loved ones, big and small, that they are precious.

For me, this is done with a special meal we make almost every year. The beauty is in the make-ahead preparation as Valentine's Day usually falls on a weekday. A table set with hints of reds and pinks with little love notes on each person's plate was something my kids always looked forward to.

French onion soup, a crisp tossed salad, lamb chops, and rice pilaf will make a special meal to start expressing that love and devotion. Here's to Prosecco, Pots de Creme, and love. Happy Valentine's Day!

ON THE
TABLE

Greek Salad with
Aunt Louise's Dressing........55

Lebanese Pilaf. 57

Slow-Cooked French
Onion Soup. 59

Marinated Lamb Chops. 61

Pots de Creme 63

Prosecco with
Strawberry Purée 64

GREEK SALAD
WITH AUNT LOUISE'S DRESSING

prep time
10 minutes, plus
30 minutes to chill

cook time
none

serves
2

Do you eat yours before or after? My grandparents would always say "When in Rome, do as the Romans," so I guess it depends if you're in Rome. I usually enjoy my salad before the meal, but eating the salad after the meal may help to cleanse the palate. Either way, this is a Greek salad that tastes delicious before, during, or after the main event, or all by itself! With Aunt Louise's dressing, it's the perfect finish to this crisp, vegetable-packed dish.

BABS SAYS...
Scale up the salad ingredients as needed. The dressing serves 4 to 6.

INGREDIENTS

2 cups salad greens of choice, torn into bite-sized pieces

1 large clove garlic

½ small cucumber, sliced

½ small red bell pepper, cored and cut into rings

¼ cup thinly sliced red onion

6 cherry tomatoes

8 pitted kalamata olives

2 oz (55g) feta cheese, cubed or crumbled

Dressing:

½ cup extra-virgin olive oil

¼ cup red wine vinegar

Juice of ½ lemon

1 tsp Dijon mustard

½ tsp salt

¼ tsp freshly ground black pepper

¼ tsp garlic powder

½ tsp dried oregano

DIRECTIONS

1. Clean the salad greens and spin dry in a salad spinner. Refrigerate for 30 minutes to chill.

2. Prepare the dressing. In a small container, whisk together all of the ingredients until thoroughly combined. Refrigerate until needed.

3. Rub the surface of the salad serving bowl with the garlic. Add the salad greens, cucumber, red pepper, red onion, and tomatoes.

4. Just before serving, add the olives and feta cheese. Pour the desired amount of dressing over the salad, toss, and serve. Store leftover dressing tightly sealed in the refrigerator for up to 1 week.

LEBANESE PILAF

prep time
5 minutes

cook time
30 minutes

serves
2–3

This is my all-time favorite rice. It's so easy to make and has such a delicious flavor with the added butter and chicken broth. I can't imagine eating plain rice when, for just a minute or two more, you can turn this side dish into a delicacy. The pignoli (pine nuts) are optional but really make it that much more special.

MAKE IT AHEAD
You can make this up to 3 days in advance, and warm in the microwave before serving. Believe it or not, I love it cold, as well!

INGREDIENTS

1–2 tbsp salted butter

1 cup dry long-grain white rice (not instant), rinsed or soaked

⅓ cup dried vermicelli noodle pieces (about ½in/1.25cm pieces)

2 tbsp pine nuts (optional)

2½ cups chicken broth

¼ cup golden raisins (optional)

¼ cup chopped flat-leaf parsley (optional)

DIRECTIONS

1. In a medium saucepan, melt the butter over medium heat. Add the rice, vermicelli, and pine nuts, and cook, stirring constantly, until golden but not brown.

2. In a heatproof bowl, heat the chicken broth in the microwave until very hot but not boiling, 2 to 3 minutes. Pour the heated broth over the rice mixture, and let it come to a full boil over medium heat.

3. Reduce the heat to low, cover, and cook for 20 minutes. Stir in the raisins and parsley (if using). Fluff the rice before serving.

SLOW-COOKED FRENCH ONION SOUP

prep time
15 minutes

cook time
4 hours

serves
6

There's just something so special about French onion soup topped with a cheese-laden, toasted baguette. There's even something more special when you can caramelize the onions and then transfer everything right into your slow cooker. This comfort food is even my granddaughter Charlotte's favorite!

INGREDIENTS

4 tbsp unsalted butter, melted

4 large yellow onions, thinly sliced into quarter moons

8 cups beef broth

½ cup dry sherry

1 tsp salt

½ tsp freshly ground black pepper

½ tsp paprika

1 tbsp Worcestershire sauce

3 sprigs fresh thyme, plus more to garnish

1 bay leaf

8 slices French baguette

2 tbsp extra-virgin olive oil, to coat the bread

½ cup grated Parmesan cheese (optional)

3 cups freshly grated Gruyère cheese

1 tbsp cognac

DIRECTIONS

1. In a large skillet or cast-iron skillet, melt the butter over low heat. Add all of the sliced onions. Cook over medium-high heat for 5 minutes. Then reduce the heat to low, and cook for 35 to 45 minutes, or until the onions are golden, stirring occasionally.

2. After the onions have caramelized, place them in a slow cooker. Cover with the beef broth, sherry, salt, pepper, paprika, Worcestershire sauce, fresh thyme, and bay leaf. Put the slow cooker on high for 3 hours.

3. When ready to serve, preheat the broiler. Brush the baguette slices with the olive oil and sprinkle with Parmesan (if using). Lightly brown the bread under the broiler, watching the cheese and bread closely so they do not burn.

4. Place broiler-proof serving bowls on a baking sheet. Remove the bay leaf and thyme stems, stir in the cognac, and fill the bowls with the soup, leaving space to top with bread. Top each bowl with a slice of toasted bread and about ⅓ cup Gruyère. Place the baking sheet under the broiler, 4 to 6 inches (10–15cm) from the broiler element. Broil for 3 to 5 minutes, or until the cheese is melted and bubbly. Watch carefully so it doesn't burn! Garnish with a few fresh thyme leaves, and serve immediately.

MAKE IT AHEAD

Prepare the soup, and store in the refrigerator for up to 3 days in advance, or freeze in an airtight container for up to 3 months. This makes it perfect for Valentine's Day. Reserve 2 servings for a romantic dinner, and freeze the rest for another special occasion! Bread can be toasted and placed in a sealed container at room temperature until ready to use, up to 2 days in advance.

MARINATED LAMB CHOPS

prep time
5 minutes, plus
2 hours for
marinating

cook time
8 minutes

serves
4

With my Lebanese heritage, lamb has always been my favorite meat. During most of the year, lamb chops were served and always prepared with a simple olive oil, lemon, and garlic marinade—an easy meal made during the week, delicious enough for company, and special enough for date night. This simple recipe has stood the test of time as one of my favorites.

INGREDIENTS

2 tbsp extra-virgin olive oil

Juice of 2 small lemons

2 tsp dried oregano

3 tbsp fresh minced garlic

1 tsp kosher salt

½ tsp freshly ground black pepper

8 loin lamb chops (about 4 oz/110g each)

DIRECTIONS

1. In a small bowl, whisk together the olive oil, lemon juice, oregano, garlic, salt, and pepper. To a large resealable or airtight container, add the lamb chops, and cover with the marinade. Seal and refrigerate for 1 to 2 hours.

2. Allow the lamb chops to come to room temperature. Preheat a grill pan on the stove, the grill, or the broiler to high heat. Grill the lamb chops for 3 to 4 minutes per side, or until an instant read thermometer registers an internal temperature of about 125°F (52°C) for medium rare. Tent loosely with foil, and let rest for 5 minutes before serving.

BABS SAYS...
To me, ruining a good piece of lamb would be to overcook it, Watch carefully.

Don't forget to serve with fresh lemon slices. They really bring the flavors to life.

ROASTED BRUSSELS SPROUTS

1 lb (450g) fresh brussels sprouts (not frozen)

2 tbsp extra-virgin olive oil

½ tsp granulated garlic

½ tsp salt, plus more to serve

¼ tsp freshly ground black pepper

1. Preheat the oven to 400°F (200°C) with the rack in the middle of the oven. Remove a few of the outer leaves of each brussels sprout, and cut the larger ones in half.

2. Into a large bowl, add the trimmed brussels sprouts, the olive oil, garlic, salt, and pepper, and toss with your hands to thoroughly coat each sprout.

3. Arrange the brussels sprouts on a large baking sheet, cut-side down. Roast for 20 to 25 minutes, or until the outer leaves are crispy and dark brown, shaking the sheet every 8 to 10 minutes for even browning. Sprinkle with a little additional salt, and serve immediately.

BABS SAYS...
About 5 minutes before the sprouts are done roasting, consider sprinkling with some grated Romano cheese or about 1 tablespoon balsamic vinegar.

POTS DE CREME

prep time
20 minutes, plus
3 hours or overnight
to chill

cook time
10 minutes

serves
6

For the past 10 years, my husband and I have been getting together with his family in Florida during the month of February. When not going out for dinner, we take turns preparing a meal for the group. My turn happened to fall on Valentine's Day. This was the make-ahead dessert that was served to the family—the perfect chocolatey end to any dinner, but especially a Valentine's one.

INGREDIENTS

2 cups heavy whipping cream

7 oz (198g) 70% cocoa dark chocolate (such as Lindt), chopped

4 large egg yolks, room temperature

¼ cup (50g) granulated sugar

1 tsp pure vanilla extract

Whipped cream, raspberries, or shaved chocolate, to serve

DIRECTIONS

1. In a medium saucepan, heat the cream over medium heat until bubbles form around the side of the pan and the cream is hot.

2. Remove from the heat. Add the chocolate and whisk until well combined and the chocolate is melted.

3. In a separate medium bowl, whisk the egg yolks, sugar, and vanilla until well combined.

4. Add a few tablespoons of the chocolate mixture to the egg mixture, whisking constantly. Add another few tablespoons, whisking constantly. Add the remaining chocolate mixture to the egg mixture, and continue whisking until well combined.

5. Pour the mixture into 6 (4 fl oz/120ml) ramekins. Cover each ramekin with plastic wrap, pressing the wrap to the surface. Refrigerate for 3 hours or overnight until cold and set. Serve topped with whipped cream, raspberries, or shaved chocolate.

BABS SAYS...

This is all about the chocolate, and no, it's definitely not pudding! Splurge on the best quality chocolate you can find. Also, use fresh eggs for this quintessential French dessert. It makes a difference!

To make chocolate curls, use a slab of high-quality chocolate. Chill the chocolate in the refrigerator before shaving. Hold the bar in one hand with a paper towel. Use a peeler to shave along the narrow length of the bar. Store the curls in the refrigerator or freezer to firm up before using.

PROSECCO
WITH STRAWBERRY PURÉE

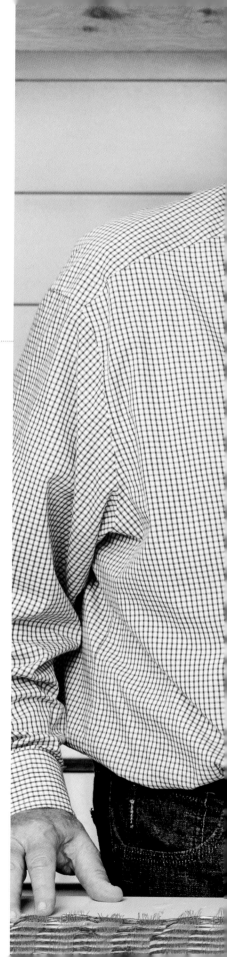

prep time
5 minutes

cook time
none

serves
6

Prosecco makes any occasion that much more special. It actually happens to be my go-to drink anytime of the year—I couldn't imagine a brunch without mimosas and Bellinis. However, for Valentine's Day, the addition of orange juice or peaches just won't cut it. Strawberries, with a touch of lemon, transforms Prosecco into the perfect Valentine's Day cocktail.

INGREDIENTS

3 fl oz (90ml) fresh lemon juice

6 servings Prosecco, very cold

6 whole strawberries, to garnish

Purée:

1 lb (450g) fresh, ripe strawberries, hulled

2 tbsp granulated sugar

DIRECTIONS

1. Make the strawberry purée. To a blender, add the strawberries and sugar. Process on high speed until smooth, 45 seconds to 1 minute. Strain the mixture through a fine-mesh sieve, and discard the seeds and pulp.

2. To each flute, add 2 tablespoons purée and ½ fluid ounce (15ml) fresh lemon juice, and stir. Top the strawberry mixture with ice-cold Prosecco. Garnish with a whole strawberry, and enjoy.

MAKE IT AHEAD

You can make the strawberry purée up to 3 days ahead of time, and store tightly sealed in the refrigerator. It will keep for 6 months frozen in an airtight container. You can even freeze the purée in ice cube trays for perfect serving sizes.

TRADITIONS TO MAKE YOUR OWN

Dress in green

Watch an old Irish film! Some of our favorites include
Darby O'Gill and the Little People, The Quiet Man, and
Waking Ned Devine

Go to a St. Patrick's Day parade

ST. PATRICK'S DAY
celebrations

My husband, Bill, is of Irish descent, so I have always made a big fuss during the month of March celebrating St. Patrick's Day. Costello is actually a very old Gaelic name, and tradition tells us that even though it sounds Italian, the Costello surname came to Ireland during the Anglo-Norman invasion in the 12th century. They go way back! So to celebrate his Irish heritage, there are certain traditions we have kept year in and year out.

I have always made soda bread, which we would eat during our traditional corned beef and cabbage meal, but also toasted in the morning with butter and jam. I've made corned beef every way imaginable throughout the years, but marinating the corned beef in apple cider and then finishing it off with the whiskey glaze is our all-time favorite. This delectable roast is always reserved for March 17th, except for the year Bill and I were invited to attend the NYC St. Patrick's Day Parade. That was the only year we ate our corned beef off schedule!

Leading up to the holiday, we played leprechaun tricks on the kids, blaming everything on elusive Liam the Leprechaun. Each year, we made a point of renting the movie *Darby O'Gill and the Little People* at our local Blockbuster. Now we share this sweet movie with our grandchildren. We introduced to them King Brian, the king of the leprechauns, and they learned about the whimsical Irish traditions that are so endearing to our family. Leading up to St. Patrick's Day, I sang every Irish song I had ever heard and taught them to the kids. In my attempt at an Irish brogue, I'd wake the kids up with "top o' the mornin' to ya," and they had to give the correct response, "and the rest of the day to yourself."

Now the highlight of St. Patrick's Day in our family is celebrating the birthdays of two of our granddaughters, Mary Elizabeth and Charlotte Aubrey. Talk about the luck of the Irish, and our luck was doublin' (but we like to refer to them as blessings)!

Just remember—everyone is Irish on St. Patrick's Day. And may the road rise to meet you, may the wind be always at your back, and may you be in heaven half an hour before the devil knows you're dead!

ON THE
TABLE

Irish Soda Bread 70

Whiskey-Glazed Corned Beef
with Cabbage 73

Guinness Cupcakes. 75

Irish Coffee. 77

Baked Reuben Casserole 79

IRISH SODA BREAD

prep time
15 minutes

cook time
35 minutes

yield
1 loaf

We have certain traditions we keep for St. Patrick's Day. Irish soda bread is one of those annual traditions. This is my son Bill's favorite food of the holiday. This is so easy to make and so heavenly served warm with butter or toasted with jam. True Irish soda bread does not have the caraway seeds or raisins, but we love the addition of both. Soaking the raisins in Jameson (the longer the better) is optional, but not for us.

INGREDIENTS

3½ cups (448g) all-purpose flour

⅓ cup (67g) granulated sugar

2 tsp caraway seeds (optional)

1 tsp baking soda

1 tsp salt

¼ cup (56g) unsalted butter, cold, cut into small cubes

1½ cups buttermilk, shaken

⅓ cup or more Jameson Irish Whiskey–soaked raisins or currants (optional), dusted with flour

DIRECTIONS

1. Preheat the oven to 400°F (200°C). In a large bowl, whisk together the flour, sugar, caraway seeds (if using), baking soda, and salt until combined.

2. To the flour mixture, add the cold cubed butter. With clean hands, work the butter into the flour mixture until the mixture resembles coarse crumbs.

3. Make a well in the center and pour in the buttermilk. Add the Jameson-soaked, flour-coated raisins (if using). Stir all of the ingredients until they come together.

4. Gather the dough and place on a floured work surface. Knead a few times until it comes into a ball. Form into a round loaf that's about 1½ inches (3.75cm) thick. If the dough is very sticky, mix in a little more flour. Don't overwork the dough. This is a quick bread.

5. Once the dough comes together, place in a greased 8- or 9-inch (20 or 23cm) round cake pan. Score an X over the top of the loaf (see Babs Says…). Bake for 30 to 35 minutes, or until golden brown. Let rest for 10 minutes, and then transfer to a wire rack to cool. Slice and serve warm or at room temperature. Store tightly wrapped at room temperature for 4 to 5 days or freeze, tightly wrapped in plastic wrap in a freezer bag, for up to 3 months.

BABS SAYS…

Make certain to use fresh baking soda because this is the leavening ingredient with the buttermilk.

I've been told that the cross is made for steam to escape and also to allow the fairies to make an exit.

MAKE IT AHEAD

Make this up to 4 days in advance. To reheat, wrap in foil and place in the oven at 200°F (95°C) until warmed through.

WHISKEY-GLAZED CORNED BEEF
WITH CABBAGE

Certain foods in life become a ritual, totally synonymous with a certain holiday. It wouldn't be St. Patrick's Day without this corned beef and cabbage. I've been making corned beef like this for years—a recipe that made its way into my old recipe box from my friend Susan. The whiskey glaze gives the cider-flavored beef a delicious fancy finish.

prep time
20 minutes, plus overnight to soak

cook time
5 hours 15 minutes

serves
6

INGREDIENTS

4–5½ lb (2–2.5 kg) flat-cut corned beef brisket with packet of brining spices (reserve the brining spices separately)

2 cups apple cider

4 large carrots, peeled and cut in 2–3in (5–7.5cm) pieces

1½ lb (680g) baby red potatoes

2 large onions, quartered

Beef broth and water, to cover (if needed)

1 small head of cabbage, cut into 8 wedges

Glaze:

¼ cup firmly packed dark brown sugar

2 tbsp whole-grain Dijon mustard

1 tbsp smooth Dijon mustard

2 tbsp Jameson Irish Whiskey

¼ tsp freshly ground black pepper

Pinch of cloves

DIRECTIONS

1. Put the brisket in an airtight container and cover with water. Refrigerate overnight to draw out salt. When ready to bake, preheat the oven to 400°F (200°C). Drain the brisket and place in a roasting pan. Pour in the apple cider and the reserved brining spices. Cover tightly with greased foil.

2. Cook for 10 minutes. Lower the temperature to 200°F (95°C) and cook for 3 hours more. At the 3-hour mark, test for fork-tenderness, and continue to cook for another hour, or until very tender. Reserve the liquid. Remove the brisket.

3. Add the reserved liquid to a large Dutch oven. Add the carrots, potatoes, and onions. Add a mixture of half beef broth and half water if more liquid is needed to cover the vegetables. Bring to a simmer over medium heat and cook for 30 to 45 minutes, until fork tender or the desired doneness. Add the cabbage wedges during the last 15 to 20 minutes of cooking.

4. Meanwhile, pat the cooked corned beef dry. Remove some of the fat from the brisket. In a small bowl, combine the glaze ingredients. Preheat the broiler. Place the brisket on a baking sheet. Lightly score the fat side of the brisket with a sharp knife in a crosshatch pattern. Brush the top and sides of the corned beef with the glaze. Place 6 to 8 inches (15–20cm) under the broiler element and broil for 4 minutes. Crack open the oven door and watch carefully to avoid burning. Repeat the glazing process 2 more times, broiling for 2 to 3 minutes each time until caramelized.

5. Let the brisket rest for 5 minutes before slicing against the grain. Serve with the veggies. Store in an airtight container in the refrigerator for up to 4 days or in the freezer for up to 3 months.

BABS SAYS...

You can cook the brisket (steps 1 and 2) in a slow cooker on low for 7 hours, or until tender. You can also use an electric pressure cooker on high for about 90 minutes, or until very tender.

If you're lucky enough to have leftovers, delicious Reuben sandwiches are awaiting, or try the Reuben Casserole (page 79).

MAKE IT AHEAD

You can make the brisket a day or two in advance (through step 2), storing in an airtight container in the refrigerator, in the liquid. When ready to serve, reheat the brisket, tightly wrapped in foil, in the oven at 300°F (150°C), and then unwrap and continue to heat for 30 minutes. Then proceed with the recipe to make the vegetables and glaze.

GUINNESS CUPCAKES

After our corned beef and cabbage dinner with all the trimmings, we would adjourn to the family room to watch for the umpteenth time *Darby O'Gill and the Little People.* Even though we knew that movie by heart, the kids would still get spooked by the banshee! As we watched that wonderful movie, these rich cupcakes would make an appearance with big glasses of cold milk. It's no surprise that these are my granddaughter Mary's favorite cupcakes—she was born on St. Patrick's Day, so it's only fitting. These are so rich and scrumptious you could make them any time!

prep time
20 minutes, plus
2 hours to cool

cook time
30 minutes

yield
24

INGREDIENTS

1 cup (224g) unsalted butter

2 cups (400g) granulated sugar

1 cup Guinness

1 tsp pure vanilla extract

2 large eggs, beaten

2 cups (256g) all-purpose flour

¾ cup (83g) cocoa powder

1½ tsp baking soda

¾ tsp salt

⅔ cup (151g) sour cream

Green sprinkles (optional), to decorate

Frosting:

1 cup (224g) salted butter, softened

2 tsp espresso powder

4 cups (460g) powdered sugar

½ tsp pure vanilla extract

2 tbsp + 1 tsp Guinness or milk

DIRECTIONS

1. Preheat the oven to 350°F (180°C). Line 2 (12-cup) muffin pans with cupcake liners. In a small saucepan, melt the unsalted butter over medium-low heat. Whisk in the granulated sugar. Whisk in the Guinness and vanilla, and remove from the heat. Whisk in the beaten eggs.

2. In the bowl of a stand mixer fitted with the paddle attachment, add the flour, cocoa, baking soda, and salt. Mix on low until well combined.

3. Slowly pour the wet ingredients into the dry ingredients, and mix on medium speed. Add the sour cream and mix on medium-low until just combined.

4. Fill the cupcake liners three-fourths full. Bake for 30 minutes, or until a toothpick inserted into the center of a cupcake comes out clean. Let stand in the pan for 10 minutes before removing to a wire rack to cool completely.

5. While the cupcakes are baking, make the frosting. In the bowl of the stand mixer fitted with the paddle attachment, cream the butter for about 2 minutes. Add the espresso powder, and mix on low speed until incorporated, scraping the sides and bottom of the bowl.

6. Add the sugar. Mix on medium speed, scraping the bottom of the bowl at least once, until well incorporated. Reduce the speed to low and add the vanilla and Guinness. Mix until incorporated. Increase the speed to medium-high and whip until light and fluffy. Be sure to scrape the bottom and sides at least once.

7. Spread or pipe the frosting onto the cooled cupcakes and decorate as desired.

BABS SAYS...
Use a piping bag and tip to get that perfect swirl, or if you don't have one, cut the corner off of a resealable zipper bag, or use an offset spatula to spread.

MAKE IT AHEAD
The cupcakes can be made and frozen (not frosted) for up to 3 months. To freeze, wrap cupcakes individually in plastic wrap and place on a baking tray in the freezer overnight. Once frozen, the cupcakes can be transferred to a resealable bag. Thaw at room temperature and decorate.

IRISH COFFEE

Believe it or not, Irish coffee did originate in Ireland. The story goes that an aircraft called "a flying boat," which was very unreliable and cumbersome, flew between Long Island, NY, and Foynes, Ireland. The cabin wasn't pressurized, so the aircraft flew very low over the ocean, making it vulnerable to weather conditions. Pilots could be halfway across the ocean and have to make a decision to either turn back or take a chance and carry on. That's exactly what happened in 1943. The flight returned to Ireland after encountering rough weather. The terminal was alerted by Morse code. They knew the passengers would be exhausted, so they called in the staff, and the chef decided the passengers needed a shot of whiskey in their coffee. The original recipe had only four ingredients. There are lots of variations on the one served that stormy night. This is our favorite. The Irish whiskey, along with the brandy and Kahlúa, give this drink a nice punch, while the vanilla whipped cream balances the alcohol. A strong coffee backbone makes for a delicious drink.

prep time
15 minutes

cook time
none

serves
4

INGREDIENTS

½ pint heavy whipping cream

1 tsp pure vanilla extract

1 tbsp light brown sugar

¼ cup powdered sugar

4 cups freshly brewed black coffee (hot!)

Whiskey mixture:
3 fl oz (90ml) Bushmills Irish Whiskey

1½ fl oz (45ml) Kahlúa

1½ fl oz (45ml) brandy

DIRECTIONS

1. In a small bowl, combine the whiskey, Kahlúa, and brandy.

2. To a medium chilled bowl, add the cream, vanilla, and sugars. Whip until very soft peaks form—thickened, but still able to pour.

3. Preheat 4 coffee mugs with hot water, letting them sit for 5 minutes with the hot water, and then empty.

4. Pour 1½ fluid ounces (45ml) whiskey mixture into each warm mug. Fill the mug three-fourths full with the hot coffee, and stir. Fill each cup to the top with the whipped cream mixture, but do not stir. Enjoy!

BABS SAYS...

If you want to be fancy, use a heated, long-handled spoon, and gently pour whipped cream mixture over the convex curve of the spoon to top up each cup. It's supposed to help the cream magically float!

BAKED REUBEN CASSEROLE

Who said you can't enjoy a Reuben on St. Patrick's Day? If you really aren't into the traditional food fare for this holiday, then this is for you. It's from my dear cousin Pam, who has never disappointed when it comes to food. Once you try this, you will never fuss making a typical Reuben again. This is far easier and so much more delicious!

prep time
20 minutes

cook time
45 minutes

serves
12

INGREDIENTS

6 slices rye bread (dark or light), divided

½ lb (225g) cooked corned beef, sliced ⅛ in (3mm) thick, chopped

½ lb (225g) pastrami, sliced ⅛ in (3mm) thick, chopped

14 oz (410g) sauerkraut, well drained

1 cup chopped sweet pickles

4 cups shredded Swiss cheese, divided

1 cup whole milk

3 large eggs, beaten

⅓ cup Thousand Island dressing

1 tbsp prepared horseradish

1 tbsp sweet pickle juice

¼ cup mustard (Dijon or yellow)

DIRECTIONS

1. Preheat the oven to 350°F (180°C). Spray a 9 x 13-inch (23 x 33cm) baking dish with nonstick cooking spray.

2. Cut 4 slices of rye bread into 2-inch (5cm) squares. Place the remaining 2 slices of bread into a food processor and pulse to make fine bread crumbs. Spread the cubed bread evenly in the bottom of the prepared dish.

3. Mix the chopped corned beef and pastrami together. Cover the bread cubes evenly with half of the chopped meat. Then evenly top with the drained sauerkraut and the chopped pickles. Sprinkle 2 cups Swiss on top of the sauerkraut layer. Top with the remaining chopped meat. Gently push down to compact the ingredients a bit. Sprinkle the remaining 2 cups Swiss on top.

4. In a medium bowl, whisk together the milk, eggs, Thousand Island dressing, horseradish, pickle juice, and mustard. Pour the mixture evenly over the casserole. Top with the bread crumbs.

5. Cover with foil and bake for 45 minutes, or until the cheese is melted and bubbly. If you like your bread crumbs toasted, remove the foil the last 10 minutes of baking. Remove from the oven and let rest for 5 minutes. Slice and serve. Keep leftovers tightly covered in the refrigerator for up to 5 days. Freeze leftovers tightly covered with plastic wrap and foil for up to 3 months.

BABS SAYS...

This is perfect using leftover Whiskey-Glazed Corned Beef (page 73) on the day after St. Patrick's Day. You could even double the corned beef and leave out the pastrami so there is no need to run to the store.

TRADITIONS TO MAKE YOUR OWN

Make Easter bread with your loved ones

Dye Easter eggs (you're never too old!)

Hide Easter baskets for a fun scavenger hunt

EASTER
luncheon

In my family growing up, the Easter season started long before Easter day. I remember as a child that the beginning of Lent was also the day my grandmother planted the reserved seeds from last year's garden. These were grown in recycled egg cartons and milk containers, lovingly cared for until warm weather was ushered in around Mother's Day. My grandmother would make her Easter pies stuffed with ricotta cheese, eggs, and homemade sweet Italian sausage, and she'd gift them to family and friends.

However, the highlight of treats was my grandmother Vincenza's homemade Easter bread. My grandmother could not read, yet she was an amazing cook, and her bread and homemade pasta and pizza were legendary. Once a year at Easter, she made each of her 22 grandchildren their very own bread doll using her sweet bread recipe. She painstakingly shaped the dough into ropes and twisted each one to form a doll, leaving an opening at the top where a colored egg was inserted for the head. I would wait a few days before I dare cut into it because I wanted to keep my doll as long as possible.

Lamb is traditionally served on Easter in an Italian-Lebanese family. My grandfather had very good friends who were Greek and owned a butcher shop in the old neighborhood. Well before Easter, my grandfather placed his lamb order. Believe me when I tell you we had the freshest, most succulent lamb in all of Chicagoland. Sometimes, Grandpa would order a whole half of a lamb. My grandmother even roasted the head! Nothing went to waste.

Many of these traditions have been passed on as we celebrate this time of year. I now make Easter sweet bread for my own grandchildren. Roasted lamb is always on the table with the addition of baked ham. Of course Easter egg hunts and hiding Easter baskets were added as we began our own family so many years ago. Easter truly is a celebration of new life.

ON THE
TABLE

Eileen's Strawberry Salad 85

Apricot Bourbon–Glazed Ham . . 87

Roasted Leg of Lamb 89

Elma's Curried Rice 91

Grandma's Easter Bread 93

Traditional Carrot Cake 94

Elaine's Champagne Punch 97

EILEEN'S STRAWBERRY SALAD

prep time
15 minutes

cook time
10 minutes

serves
8

This is my daughter Elizabeth's absolute favorite spring and summertime salad. Her mother-in-law Eileen serves this at every springtime holiday, family barbecue, and get-together. It's her most requested recipe ever— one taste and you'll know why. It's easy to prepare, and the inclusion of the ramen noodles is a great unexpected, crunchy addition.

INGREDIENTS

1 (3 oz/85g) pkg dried ramen noodles, crushed

¼ cup sliced raw almonds

¼ cup sunflower seeds

¼ cup unsalted butter, melted

1 large head romaine lettuce, washed and dried

5 oz (140g) arugula or baby spinach

1 pint (12 oz) strawberries, hulled and thinly sliced

1 cup grated Parmesan cheese

Dressing:

½ cup granulated sugar

½ cup red wine vinegar

¾ cup extra-virgin olive oil

½ tsp paprika

½ tsp kosher salt

3 cloves garlic, minced

DIRECTIONS

1. Preheat the oven to 350°F (180°C). In a small bowl, mix the ramen noodles, almonds, sunflower seeds, and melted butter. Transfer to a baking dish and toast in the oven, stirring occasionally, until browned, about 10 minutes. Remove from the oven and set aside to cool.

2. Tear the romaine lettuce into bite-sized pieces. In a large bowl, combine the lettuce, arugula, strawberries, and Parmesan. Cover and refrigerate.

3. Prepare the dressing. In a small bowl, dissolve the sugar in the vinegar. Add the oil, paprika, salt, and garlic, and mix well.

4. Just before serving, sprinkle the crunchy topping over the salad mixture and toss with just enough dressing to coat the greens. Make sure not to overdress the salad. Serve immediately. Reserve leftover dressing in an airtight container in the refrigerator for up to 1 week.

BABS SAYS...

If almonds and sunflower seeds are not your favorites, experiment with the nuts you prefer.

MAKE IT AHEAD

The dressing may be made ahead and stored in the refrigerator until ready to serve. (You will have plenty of leftover dressing to be enjoyed for another purpose.) The salad ingredients can also be combined and refrigerated ahead of time—but leave the crunchy bits separate until ready to serve.

APRICOT BOURBON-GLAZED HAM

prep time
20 minutes

cook time
2 hours 30 minutes

serves
10–12

A few years back, my good friend shared her longtime family recipe for glazed ham with me. The apricot nectar really takes it to the next level. This is so flavorful and easy to make, and serves a crowd. It has been on our menu every year since. It's perfect for a large family—all my kids still look for leftovers to serve their own families the next day. Leftovers can be used in so many ways, from split pea soup to ham sandwiches.

INGREDIENTS

7–9 lb (3–4kg) bone-in, precooked, spiral-cut ham

15 whole cloves

25 fl oz (740ml) apricot nectar

1 cup apricot preserves

½ cup firmly packed light brown sugar

2 tbsp bourbon

1 tbsp Dijon mustard

DIRECTIONS

1. Let the ham come to room temperature. Preheat the oven to 325°F (170°C). Score the fat in a crosshatch pattern, and place a clove at each intersection.

2. Line a large roasting pan with foil. Place the ham in the roasting pan, flat side down. Pour the apricot nectar over the ham. Cover the pan tightly with foil. Bake the ham for 12 to 15 minutes per pound, or until the internal temperature reaches 125 to 130°F (52–54°C).

3. While the ham is cooking, make the glaze. In a small saucepan, combine the apricot preserves, brown sugar, bourbon, and mustard. Bring to a boil over medium heat. Reduce the heat and let the glaze simmer for 1 to 2 minutes, stirring occasionally.

4. When the ham reaches the correct internal temperature, remove from the oven and take off the foil. Brush the glaze over the top and between the slices of the ham.

5. Return the pan to the oven, uncovered, and cook until it reaches an internal temperature of 140°F (60°C).

6. Remove from the oven, cover the ham loosely with foil, and let rest for 10 minutes before serving. Remove the cloves before serving. After removing the ham from the bone, leftovers can be stored in an airtight container in the refrigerator for up to 5 days or in the freezer for up to 3 months.

BABS SAYS...
Boneless hams are easier to cut, but a bone-in ham is going to be more flavorful. Take your pick!

This can be made in a slow cooker. Cook on low for 4 to 5 hours, or until the internal temperature reaches 140°F (60°C). Baste with the glaze every 45 minutes.

ROASTED LEG OF LAMB

With my Middle Eastern and Italian heritage, I couldn't imagine Easter without roasted lamb on the table. Lamb is truly a comfort food for me. Our roasted leg of lamb was seasoned using salt, pepper, a little olive oil and oregano, and a lot of garlic, with an added splash of wine. I started marinating my lamb using these basic ingredients several years ago. I usually roast this in the oven, but occasionally I roast it on a spit. Either way, it's a simple, delicious entrée that is a spring family tradition.

prep time
10 minutes, plus
8 hours or overnight
to marinate

cook time
2–3 hours

serves
8

INGREDIENTS

Juice of 1 lemon

1 cup dry white wine

½ cup extra-virgin olive oil

3 cloves garlic, minced

2 tsp chopped fresh rosemary leaves

1 tsp dried oregano

1 tsp chopped fresh thyme leaves

1 tsp sea salt

¼ tsp freshly ground black pepper

5–6 lb (2.25–2.75kg) bone-in leg of lamb, trimmed of fat

4 cloves garlic, thinly sliced

DIRECTIONS

1. In a medium bowl, stir together the lemon juice and wine. Slowly drizzle in the olive oil, constantly whisking to emulsify. Stir in the minced garlic, rosemary, oregano, and thyme. Allow to rest for 10 minutes. Place the lamb in a large bowl. Rub the lamb with the salt and pepper. Pour the marinade over the lamb, and rub well. Cover tightly with plastic wrap, and refrigerate for 8 hours or overnight, turning occasionally.

2. When ready to roast, remove the plastic wrap and allow the lamb to come to room temperature. Preheat the oven to 400°F (200°C). Wipe the lamb dry, and reserve the marinade for basting. Cut 1-inch- (2.50cm) deep incisions all over the lamb. Insert a slice of fresh garlic into each slit. Place the lamb fat-side up on a rack in a large roasting pan. Roast the lamb for 30 minutes.

3. Turn the lamb fat-side down, and reduce the heat to 325°F (170°C). Baste with the reserved marinade, and continue to cook until you reach the desired internal temperature, basting every 15 minutes. Insert the thermometer into the meaty part of the lamb, making sure not to touch the bone. For medium rare, roast until the internal temperature reaches 135 to 145°F (57–63°C), or 20 to 25 minutes per pound. For medium, roast until the internal temperature reaches 160°F (71°C), or 25 to 30 minutes per pound. For well done, roast until the internal temperature reaches 170°F (77°C), or 30 to 35 minutes per pound.

4. Place the lamb on a cutting board, reserving the juices in the pan. Cover the roast loosely with foil, and let rest for 20 minutes. To serve, cut into thin slices against the grain.

BABS SAYS...

Make sure the butcher removes the papery tissue covering the lamb, called the fell.

If you'd like to cook the lamb on a spit, roast it for 35 minutes per pound for medium rare, or until it reaches the desired temperature.

Skim the fat from the juices, and season the juices with salt and pepper to serve on the side. I love mint jelly with my lamb, too!

ELMA'S CURRIED RICE

The first time I had this cold curried rice salad was at a church picnic. Everyone shared a dish, and this was Elma's contribution. It is the perfect side dish to take to a picnic or barbecue, or place on the Easter table. Not only is it colorful, but it is also able to be made a day or two ahead of time. Once you taste this, you'll become as obsessed with it as I am. Just be ready to share the recipe!

prep time
5 minutes, plus overnight to chill

cook time
30 minutes

serves
12

BABS SAYS...
Dress this salad an hour or two before serving so the flavors marry.

You can substitute dried cranberries or dried apricots for the raisins.

INGREDIENTS

1 cup dry long-grain rice

1 (6 oz/170g) box herbed long-grain and wild rice mix (such as Ben's Original)

1 green bell pepper, chopped

1 red bell pepper, chopped

2 small bunches green onions, white and green parts chopped

1 (15 oz/420g) box of raisins

1 (12 oz/340g) can roasted, salted peanuts

1 (10 oz/285g) bag frozen peas

Dressing:

½ cup extra-virgin olive oil

¼ cup honey

¼ cup white wine vinegar

1 tbsp curry powder

DIRECTIONS

1. Cook both of the rices according to directions on the packages. Make sure to add the herb mixture to the wild rice. Allow to cool.

2. In a large bowl, combine the cooled rice, bell peppers, onions, and raisins. Cover and refrigerate overnight.

3. The next day, stir in the peanuts and frozen peas.

4. In a small bowl, whisk together all of the ingredients for the dressing. Pour over the salad and thoroughly mix. Serve chilled. Leftovers can be stored in an airtight container in the refrigerator for 2 to 3 days before the salad loses its crunch.

GRANDMA'S EASTER BREAD

prep time
15 minutes, plus
about 2 hours
for rising

cook time
25 minutes

yield
6

My grandmother had 22 grandchildren. Every holiday, my dear grandmother made each grandchild an Easter "doll" made of bread with an egg for the head. This tradition was carried on for years, until her grandchildren became adults, and then the great-grandchildren received these precious gifts made with pure love. I've simplified this, and now I make Easter wreaths for my grandchildren. And so it goes...

INGREDIENTS

1 (¼ oz/2¼ tsp) pkg instant dry yeast

1¼ cups whole milk, warmed

Pinch of kosher salt

⅓ cup (75g) unsalted butter, room temperature

½ cup (100g) granulated sugar

½ tsp pure vanilla extract

1 tsp lemon zest

3 large eggs, room temperature, divided

3½–4½ cups (448–576g) all-purpose flour, divided

Sprinkles, to decorate

6 raw, dyed Easter eggs (see Babs Says...)

DIRECTIONS

1. To the bowl of a stand mixer fitted with the paddle attachment, combine the yeast, milk, salt, butter, sugar, vanilla, lemon zest, and 2 eggs. Mix on medium speed until combined.

2. Switch to the dough hook attachment. Add 1¾ cups (224g) flour and mix, working the flour into the egg mixture. Mix in more flour, a little at a time, until the dough is no longer sticky, up to 2¾ cups (352g) more flour.

3. Turn the dough onto a lightly floured work surface and knead it for 1 to 2 minutes. Place in a lightly greased bowl and cover with plastic wrap. Place the dough in a warm spot to rise until doubled in size, about 1 hour.

4. Punch down the dough and divide into 12 equal pieces. Roll each piece into a rope about 14 inches (36cm) long and 1 inch (2.5cm) wide.

5. Take two ropes and twist together. Then with the twist, form a circle. Repeat to make 6 circle "wreaths." Place the wreaths on a parchment-lined baking sheet.

6. Cover with plastic wrap, place in a warm spot, and let rise until doubled in size, about 1 hour.

7. Preheat the oven to 350°F (180°C). In a small bowl, whisk together the remaining 1 egg with 1 teaspoon water. After the wreaths have doubled in size, brush with the egg wash. Sprinkle with the sprinkles. Place a dyed egg in the center of each wreath.

8. Bake for 20 to 25 minutes, or until the wreath is golden brown. Enjoy warm or room temperature.

BABS SAYS...
To dye your eggs, mix ½ cup boiling water with 1 teaspoon white vinegar and 10 to 20 drops food coloring. Submerge the eggs in the dye for about 5 minutes.

The raw eggs will cook in the oven—no need to hard-boil them first!

MAKE IT AHEAD
Prepare the dough up to 1 day in advance, and store tightly covered in the refrigerator. Just let it come to room temperature, and then shape into wreaths. You can also shape into wreaths first, and then refrigerate. Remove from the refrigerator and let the dough rest until doubled in size.

The dough can be frozen as wreaths before or after baking. If freezing the dough after baking, make sure to remove the egg.

TRADITIONAL CARROT CAKE

prep time
20 minutes

cook time
45 minutes

serves
8–10

This is my go-to carrot cake. There are not a lot of bells and whistles, but it's the most moist, carrot-filled cake I've ever made. For Easter, I make it in my mom's vintage lamb cake mold and decorate with shredded coconut for the fleece, jelly beans for the eyes, and a little ribbon collar. It always goes so extremely fast that I make a second cake, as well. The cool cream cheese frosting is a must for this all-American traditional dessert.

INGREDIENTS

2 cups (256g) all-purpose flour

2 tsp baking powder

2 tsp ground cinnamon

1 tsp salt

4 large eggs, room temperature

1¼ cups vegetable oil

2 cups (400g) granulated sugar

3 cups (348g) grated carrots

Frosting:

8 oz (225g) cream cheese, room temperature

½ cup (112g) salted butter, room temperature

1 lb (450g) powdered sugar, sifted

1 tsp pure vanilla extract

DIRECTIONS

1. Preheat the oven to 350°F (180°C). Grease 2 (9-inch/23cm) round cake pans. In a medium bowl, combine the flour, baking powder, cinnamon, and salt.

2. In a large bowl, whisk together the eggs, oil, and sugar until smooth. Stir in the flour mixture and carrots.

3. Pour the batter evenly into the prepared cake pans. Bake for 40 to 45 minutes, or until a toothpick inserted into the center comes out clean. Cool in the pans for 10 minutes, and then remove the cakes from the pan and cool completely on a rack.

4. While the cakes are cooling, prepare the frosting. In the bowl of a stand mixer fitted with the paddle attachment, combine the cream cheese and butter on medium-high speed until light and fluffy. Gradually add the powdered sugar, beating well. Beat in the vanilla. Continue beating until it's a spreadable consistency. Decorate the cake.

5. Store the cake, covered, in the refrigerator for up to 5 days. The frosted cake may be frozen for up to 2 months, wrapped in plastic and foil. Thaw in the refrigerator the day before you need it. Loosen the wrap, allowing the cake to warm up slowly so the naturally moist cake doesn't become mushy.

BABS SAYS...
As a decorative element, add little squiggly carrots to the outside of the cake.

MAKE IT AHEAD
This cake can be baked a day ahead and frosted the next day. Just wrap the unfrosted layers in plastic wrap and store at room temperature. The unfrosted cake may also be frozen for up to 2 months—wrap each layer separately in plastic wrap, and then wrap in foil.

ELAINE'S CHAMPAGNE PUNCH

My mom was a hairdresser and practiced her art until she was well into her 70s. Elaine was one of her dearest customers who faithfully arrived weekly in Minnie's basement salon for coffee and a chat while she was being beautified. Not only was Elaine a dear friend, she was also a wonderful cook who shared many recipes with my mom. This effervescent punch is one we have enjoyed for many a holiday.

prep time
5 minutes

cook time
none

serves
24

INGREDIENTS

2 (750ml) bottles dry sparkling wine, chilled

½ (750ml) bottle apricot brandy

1 liter (1 qt) chilled club soda

Raspberries (optional), to garnish

DIRECTIONS

1. In a large pitcher or punch bowl, mix all ingredients together. Serve chilled with raspberries to garnish (if using).

BABS SAYS...

If using a punch bowl, float strawberries on top.

Make a beautiful ice ring for the punch bowl. Freeze edible flowers and mint in a bundt pan. For a clear ice mold, do not use tap water—use distilled water that has been boiled and cooled twice.

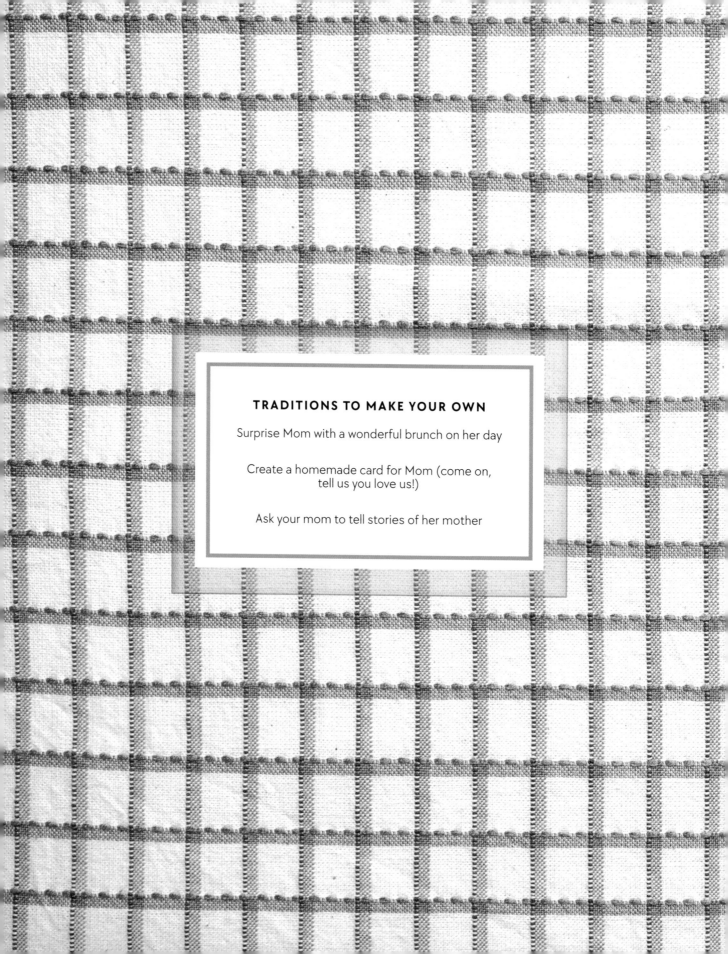

TRADITIONS TO MAKE YOUR OWN

Surprise Mom with a wonderful brunch on her day

Create a homemade card for Mom (come on,
tell us you love us!)

Ask your mom to tell stories of her mother

MOTHER'S DAY
brunch

Brunch for Mother's Day is the ultimate celebration for me. When the kids were young, I would awaken to fresh flowers, handmade cards of love, and breakfast in bed. Now the family unites late in the morning to enjoy the day to honor Mom. I feel like I was made to be a mom. Of all the different hats I wear in life, the hat of motherhood is my most rewarding. It's so hard to explain, but when a child comes into your life, you change forever. Yes, your life takes on a whole new dimension, but the rewards so outweigh any of the sacrifices. I have always said that you are the best mom for the child in front of you. It's not by chance they call *you*, and you alone, Mother. So this day is set aside, one day a year to officially lavish Mom with love and attention for all she does each and every day to keep the family afloat.

Even now as a grandmother, I often think of the sacrifices my own mother and so many of our mothers made for us, and their mothers for them. My grandmother, Vincenza, left Italy as a 20-year-old woman, never to see her own parents again. She came to this country to marry my grandfather, Luigi, and to find a better life for both herself and her future generations. Nine children and 22 grandchildren later, I was honored to have been able to call her Grandma.

My own mom had an 8th grade education. She couldn't go to high school because she was home helping her mom with the younger children. With only an elementary education, she became a very successful business woman and excelled at anything she tried. From managing her own hair salon, to owning a restaurant, and in her retirement years, starting a craft business, Minnie had an invincible can-do attitude. Whatever she put her mind to, she did with gusto and perfection.

There are many types of mother figures in life, and this day is for lavishing appreciation on anyone who has loved and cared for you. My perfect day to celebrate motherhood is enjoying my favorite meal of the day with my family...brunch! And my favorite brunch includes French toast, a bacon and egg casserole, a delicious salad, easy cinnamon rolls, an Italian cream cake, and my drink of choice—mimosas. Here's to mothers and Mother's Day!

ON THE
TABLE

Mixed Greens Salad 103

French Toast
Overnight Casserole. 105

Perfect Egg Brunch
Casserole. 107

Cheater's Pecan
Cinnamon Rolls 109

Italian Cream Cake. 111

Elderflower Mimosas 112

MIXED GREENS SALAD

prep time
15 minutes

cook time
none

serves
6

This is a simple, light, green salad with a classic French dressing that complements any meal. It's especially good when serving a variety of holiday foods because of its clean, crisp taste.

INGREDIENTS

1 romaine heart

1 clove garlic

5 oz (140g) arugula

2 medium cucumbers

Croutons (optional), to serve (store-bought or see Babs Says...)

Dressing:

6 tbsp extra-virgin olive oil

2 tbsp red wine vinegar

Juice of ½ lemon

½ tsp kosher salt

½ tsp ground mustard

Freshly ground black pepper, to taste

DIRECTIONS

1. Wash the romaine. Shake well to get rid of excess moisture, or run through a salad spinner. Tear the leaves into bite-sized pieces.

2. Rub a large salad bowl with the clove of garlic. Add the romaine and arugula.

3. Cut off the tips of the cucumber. With a fork, score deep lengthwise grooves around the cucumbers. Cut them into fairly thin slices—the edges will be fluted. Mix the cucumber slices with the salad greens.

4. In a small bowl, stir together all of the ingredients for the dressing.

5. When ready to serve, stir the dressing vigorously and pour the desired amount over the salad. You will not need all the dressing—reserve leftovers tightly sealed in the refrigerator for up to 1 week.

6. Top the salad with croutons (if using), and toss lightly. Serve immediately.

BABS SAYS...

Add grilled chicken or roasted salmon to transform this light salad into a lovely entrée.

To make your own croutons, cut 2 slices of ciabatta bread into cubes. In a medium skillet, heat 2 tablespoons oil and a small whole clove of garlic until hot. Add the bread to crisp, stirring often, until the bread cubes are golden on all sides. Drain on paper towels.

FRENCH TOAST OVERNIGHT CASSEROLE

When our older daughter, Erin, was attending Miami of Ohio, Bill and I would stay at the Gunkel Heritage Bed and Breakfast for Parent's Weekend. This was a lovely, intimate, 1800s home in Germantown. The family warmly welcomed us each time we had the pleasure of staying there. The highlight of our visit was the amazing breakfasts awaiting us each morning. One of our favorite dishes was their overnight French toast, served with melted butter and warm maple syrup. This dish is inspired by those memorable breakfasts.

prep time
15 minutes, plus overnight to soak

cook time
30 minutes

serves
8

BABS SAYS...
Dust with powdered sugar and serve with sliced strawberries. Heavenly!

INGREDIENTS

1 cup brown sugar

½ cup unsalted butter

2 tbsp pure maple syrup

5 large eggs

2 cups heavy cream or whole milk

1 tsp pure vanilla extract

½ tsp ground cinnamon (optional)

¼ tsp ground nutmeg (optional)

1 loaf French or Italian bread, cut into 2in (5cm) cubes

Powdered sugar, sliced strawberries, butter, and pure maple syrup, to serve

DIRECTIONS

1. The day before serving, in a small saucepan, melt the brown sugar, butter, and maple syrup over low heat, stirring until combined.

2. Spray a 9 x 13-inch (23 x 33cm) casserole dish with nonstick cooking spray. Pour the sugar mixture into the prepared dish.

3. In a medium bowl, beat the eggs, cream, vanilla, and cinnamon and nutmeg (if using) until combined. Add the bread cubes, and toss to coat well. Arrange the mixture in the prepared dish. Cover and refrigerate overnight.

4. Preheat the oven to 350°F (180°C). Let the casserole come to room temperature before baking. Bake, uncovered, for 30 minutes, or until browned and the egg is set. Let cool for a few minutes, and then slice and serve with the desired toppings. Store, covered, in the refrigerator for up to 3 days, or frozen in an airtight container for up to 3 months.

PERFECT EGG BRUNCH CASSEROLE

prep time
30 minutes

cook time
35 minutes

serves
10–12

I remember when I first tasted this unique brunch casserole at a lady's luncheon in Midlothian, Virginia. I thought this was one of the most delicious ways I had ever been served bacon and eggs. There is layer upon layer of a silky cream sauce, lightly seasoned with a medley of herbs, draped over the sliced hard-boiled eggs, sprinkled with bacon, and topped with just a touch of buttered bread crumbs. This is one of the most delicious brunch casseroles I have ever had! You won't be disappointed.

INGREDIENTS

¼ cup butter

¼ cup all-purpose flour

1 cup heavy whipping cream

1 cup whole milk

¼ tsp dried thyme

¼ tsp dried basil

¼ tsp dried marjoram

¼ tsp dried chervil

1 tsp salt

1 lb (450g) sharp cheddar cheese, grated

1½ dozen hard-boiled eggs (see Babs Says...), sliced

1 lb (450g) crumbled bacon

¼ cup finely chopped fresh flat-leaf parsley

Buttered fresh bread crumbs (1–1½ cups; see Babs Says...)

DIRECTIONS

1. Preheat the oven to 350°F (180°C). Create a roux. In a small saucepan, cook the butter and flour over medium heat, whisking constantly, for 1 minute. While continuing to whisk to make sure the sauce doesn't scorch, slowly pour in the cream and milk. Keep whisking until the sauce thickens and begins to boil.

2. Once boiling, decrease the heat to low. Stir in the thyme, basil, marjoram, chervil, salt, and cheese. Stir until the cheese is completely melted. Add more liquid if needed to thin. Remove from the heat.

3. In a 2-quart (2L) casserole dish, spread a thin layer of the cheese sauce. Then add a layer of one-third of the hard-boiled egg slices. Sprinkle one-third of the bacon over the eggs, followed by one-third of the chopped parsley. Repeat to add two more layers, using up all of the remaining ingredients.

4. Top with a light, even layer of buttered bread crumbs. Bake, uncovered, for 25 to 30 minutes, or until the casserole is bubbling. Let cool for a few minutes, and then slice and serve.

BABS SAYS...

I have found steaming eggs to hard-boil works like a charm, and the shells almost fall off by themselves. Put an inch of water in a medium pan with a steamer basket. Cover and bring to a boil. Add the eggs in a single layer. Cover and cook over high heat for 12 minutes. Remove the eggs from heat and submerge in an ice water bath to cool completely, about 10 minutes.

To make fresh bread crumbs, use about 3 slices heavy white bread. Remove the crusts. Pulse the slices in a food processor. In a sauté pan, melt 3 tablespoons butter over medium heat. Toss in the bread crumbs and toast until golden.

MAKE IT AHEAD

You can hard-boil the eggs ahead of time, but slice right before using.

Prepare the cheese sauce and fry the bacon up to a day in advance.

CHEATER'S PECAN CINNAMON ROLLS

prep time
15 minutes

cook time
25 minutes

serves
8

I make pecan rolls from scratch, but when I just don't have the time and still want to enjoy a delicious pecan cinnamon roll, here's my tried-and-true shortcut. I know it's cheating, but sometimes you just have to. The gooey caramel nut topping cascading over the rolls is not the shortcut part!

INGREDIENTS

½ cup salted butter

1 cup firmly packed light brown sugar

¼ cup honey

1½ cups coarsely chopped pecans

2 (12 oz/340g) tubes cinnamon rolls with glaze topping (16 rolls)

DIRECTIONS

1. Preheat the oven to 375°F (190°C). Grease a 9-inch (23cm) square baking dish.

2. In a small saucepan, melt the butter over medium heat. Add the brown sugar and honey, stirring until smooth. Bring to a full boil, and stir constantly for 1 minute. Pour the mixture evenly into the prepared pan.

3. Top evenly with the pecans. Arrange the rolls in the pan in four rows of four.

4. Bake for 20 to 25 minutes, or until the rolls are browned and the caramel layer is bubbling. Remove from the oven and cool in the pan for a few minutes.

5. Carefully invert the pecan rolls onto a platter. While still hot, cover with the glazed topping from the package (if desired). Enjoy immediately.

MAKE IT AHEAD
Cook these up to 2 days in advance, without the premade glaze topping, storing tightly covered in the refrigerator. Reheat in the oven at 375°F (190°C) until hot all the way through.

ITALIAN CREAM CAKE

prep time
35 minutes,
plus chilling

cook time
30 minutes

serves
12 or more

This is the queen of all cakes. If you love a rich, decadent cake filled with coconut and toasted pecans, this is that cake. I'm not sure what southern state takes credit for this delectable creation, but rumor has it an Italian baker living in one of the US southern states invented it in the 1900s. I was introduced to this recipe by a dear friend in Richmond. There are a few steps involved, but the effort is so worth it. Treat your mom to this unforgettable dessert, and she will wish every day was Mother's Day!

INGREDIENTS

Cake:

5 large eggs, room temperature, separated

2 cups (256g) all-purpose flour, plus more to coat

1 tsp baking soda

½ tsp salt

½ cup (90g) shortening, such as Spectrum

½ cup (112g) unsalted butter, softened, plus more to grease

2 cups (400g) granulated sugar

2 tsp pure vanilla extract

1 cup buttermilk

2 cups (170g) sweetened, shredded coconut, plus more to decorate

1 cup (120g) coarsely chopped, toasted pecans

Frosting:

8 oz (225g) cream cheese, softened

½ cup (112g) unsalted butter, softened

1 tsp pure vanilla extract

1 lb (450g) powdered sugar

1 cup (120g) chopped, toasted pecans (or left whole for decoration)

DIRECTIONS

1. Preheat the oven to 350°F (180°C). Lightly butter and flour (or use nonstick cooking spray) 3 (9-inch/23cm) round cake pans. Prepare the cake. In the bowl of a stand mixer fitted with the paddle attachment, beat the egg whites on high speed until stiff peaks form. Set aside in a separate bowl. In a large bowl, sift together the flour, baking soda, and salt.

2. In the bowl of the cleaned stand mixer, cream together the shortening, butter, sugar, and vanilla on medium-high speed until light and fluffy, 3 to 4 minutes.

3. With the motor running, add the 5 egg yolks one at a time, beating well after each addition to thoroughly incorporate.

4. With the motor running on medium-low speed, alternate adding in the sifted dry ingredients and the buttermilk until thoroughly combined.

5. Stir in the shredded coconut and pecans. Gently fold in the stiffly beaten egg whites. Portion the batter evenly into the 3 prepared pans. Bake for 30 minutes, or until a toothpick inserted into the center comes out clean.

6. While the cake is baking, prepare the frosting. In the bowl of the stand mixer, cream together the cream cheese and butter on medium speed until light and fluffy. Beat in the vanilla. Gradually beat in the powdered sugar until the icing is creamy and smooth. Fold in the chopped pecans, or reserve for decorating on top.

7. Decorate the cake. Spread frosting between the layers and on top and around the side of the cake. Decorate with additional coconut flakes and pecans (if using). Chill fully before serving.

BABS SAYS...
This is very rich—and so delicious—so slice in small servings.

MAKE IT AHEAD
This cake is best made 1 day in advance. As it rests in the refrigerator, it gets even better. Store covered while it chills.

ELDERFLOWER MIMOSAS

No surprise here that my favorite meal of the day is brunch, and my absolute favorite brunch of the year is on Mother's Day. Everything just has to be extra special, including taking your typical brunch drink to the next level. This is a delicious twist on the traditional mimosa, using the light, sweet floral taste of St. Germain Elderflower liqueur. Once you try this, you might never go back to the original.

prep time
2 minutes

cook time
none

yield
1

INGREDIENTS

1½ fl oz (45ml) St. Germain Elderflower Liqueur (see Babs Says…)

½ fl oz (15ml) orange juice

Very cold Prosecco, to top it off

DIRECTIONS

1. In a champagne flute, add all of the ingredients in the order listed. Enjoy!

BABS SAYS…

St. Germain Liqueur is made from the elderberry flowers grown on the hillside of the French Alps. Because it is made without preservatives, it should be consumed within 6 months of opening for best flavor. Store it in the refrigerator; plus it tastes delightful when chilled.

TRADITIONS TO MAKE YOUR OWN

Serve the birthday person breakfast in bed

Let your birthday girl or boy pick their favorite meal
for dinner

Decorate their room with balloons
while they are fast asleep

BIRTHDAY CAKE
bash

One of my earliest memories as a child was attending my Uncle Ralph's birthday party. He wasn't really my uncle, but he was a *cumba*, in Italian meaning a very close friend or a godfather. Out of respect, the kids would call all these close friends uncles or aunts. Uncle Ralph greeted us at the door, decked out in full cowboy attire. There were presents everywhere. It looked like Christmas. I had no idea that those presents were actually for the kids. I was the youngest there, and I waited patiently for my name to be called so I could go up to Uncle Ralph and receive my gift. When my name was finally called, I was on the verge of tears as I received the very last gift, a real tea set. That happened over 65 years ago, and that gesture by Uncle Ralph left an indelible memory. Birthdays are about making people feel loved and special. Uncle Ralph did a reverse on us.

Years later, as my own children grew up, the birthdays began with breakfast in bed (even if it was a school day)—a stack of piping hot pancakes, the number corresponding to the year being celebrated, was served on a platter with candles all aglow. This was their first birthday cake of the week. Yes, we celebrated birthdays for a solid week! There was their school party, the friend party, the family party, and last but not least, their special celebration at El Toritos, a local Mexican restaurant where mariachis sang to the birthday *panchito* or *panchita*.

As we now celebrate the grandchildren's birthdays, we've added funfetti cake to the traditional selections. Gone are the days when a cupcake is given to a one-year-old to go at. Now, our tradition is their very own smash cake. As the years continue, our birthday celebrations have been tweaked, but the idea of lavishing love on the birthday child continues.

Birthdays have always held such a special place in my heart. Every year my children would plan out their entire birthday menus, with their favorite foods at every meal on their special days—the most important item always being the cake! All my children love chocolate cake, and then my youngest came along with her favorite being a rainbow sprinkle vanilla cake. (The youngest always changes it up for the family, don't they?!) Either way, whether you are more of a chocolate or vanilla lover, I included recipes for both of our favorites here. They are delicious and easy to make, and your family will enjoy them for years to come.

ON THE
TABLE

Ford's Perfect
Chocolate Cake 118

Rainbow Sprinkle
Funfetti Cake 119

Vanilla Buttercream Frosting . . .120

Smash Cake. 121

Pancake Breakfast. 122

FORD'S PERFECT CHOCOLATE CAKE

prep time
20 minutes,
plus cooling

cook time
35 minutes

serves
12

This is one very special cake that we only serve for birthdays; however, it is easy enough to make for a midweek treat. If you have a chocolate lover in your family, this is their cake. Our chocoholic, my grandson Ford, gives this two thumbs up! It's the quintessential celebratory cake that only needs the candles.

INGREDIENTS

2 cups (256g) all-purpose flour

2 cups (400g) granulated sugar

¾ cup (83g) cocoa powder

2 tsp baking soda

1½ tsp baking powder

1 tsp salt

1 cup whole milk

½ cup vegetable oil

2 large eggs

2 tsp pure vanilla extract

1 cup coffee (or boiling water)

Frosting:

1 cup (170g) semi-sweet chocolate chips

½ cup half-and-half

1 cup (224g) unsalted butter

2½ cups (568g) powdered sugar, sifted

1 tsp pure vanilla extract

DIRECTIONS

1. Preheat the oven to 350°F (180°C). Prepare 2 (9-inch/23cm) cake pans by spraying with baking spray or greasing and lightly flouring. (Be sure to shake out excess flour.)

2. To the bowl of a stand mixer fitted with the whisk attachment, add the flour, sugar, cocoa powder, baking soda, baking powder, and salt. Whisk to thoroughly combine.

3. To the flour mixture, add the milk, oil, eggs, and vanilla. Mix on medium speed until well combined. (The mixture will be thick.)

4. Boil the coffee. Reduce the mixer speed to low and slowly add the boiling coffee to the batter. After all the coffee is added, bring the speed up to high, and beat for about 1 minute.

5. Evenly distribute the batter between the prepared cake pans. Bake for 30 to 35 minutes, or until a toothpick inserted in the center comes out clean. Cool in the pans on a cooling rack for 15 minutes. Then quickly flip the cakes onto the rack to invert and remove the pan.

6. Make the frosting. In a small saucepan over medium-low heat, melt together the chocolate, half-and-half, and butter until smooth. Set aside and cool for 15 minutes. Once cooled, place in the bowl of a stand mixer fitted with the paddle attachment. Add the powdered sugar and vanilla. Beat on high for 5 to 7 minutes, or until the frosting is creamy and light in color. You will have plenty of frosting for a double-layer cake.

7. Allow the cakes to cool completely before frosting and decorating (page 120).

BABS SAYS...
Drape a kitchen towel over your mixer, covering the entire head and bowl to avoid splatter. If you also have a splatter shield, even better—drape the towel over that, too!

Crack your eggs in a separate bowl first to avoid getting any shell in the batter.

MAKE IT AHEAD
Freeze this cake for up to 3 months. Place in the freezer, uncovered, for 1 hour to set the frosting. Then wrap the cake in a double layer of plastic wrap, followed by aluminum foil. Thaw in the refrigerator the day before serving.

RAINBOW SPRINKLE FUNFETTI CAKE

Rainbows, unicorns, and this rainbow sprinkle cake are just a few of my granddaughter Finley's favorite things. This is the quintessential birthday cake and a family favorite! This super moist, yummy Rainbow Sprinkle Funfetti Cake is like a colorful party all rolled up in a cake. Take one bite and you'll know exactly what I mean!

prep time
30 minutes,
plus cooling

cook time
40 minutes

serves
12

INGREDIENTS

½ cup (112g) unsalted butter, softened

3 cups (600g) granulated sugar

1 cup vegetable oil

4 tsp pure vanilla extract

4 cups + 2 tbsp (528g) all-purpose flour

4½ tsp baking powder

1½ tsp salt

1½ cups whole milk

9 egg whites, room temperature

⅔ cup + 2 tbsp (152g) rainbow jimmies, divided (see Babs Says...), plus more to decorate

Vanilla Buttercream Frosting (page 120)

DIRECTIONS

1. Preheat the oven to 350°F (180°C). Prepare the pans of your choice (see Babs Says...) by spraying with baking spray or greasing and lightly flouring. In a stand mixer fitted with the paddle attachment, beat the butter on medium to medium-high speed until creamy, scraping the bowl as necessary. Add the sugar and oil. Beat until creamy and fluffy. Scrape down the sides of the bowl as necessary. Mix in the vanilla.

2. In a separate medium bowl, whisk together the flour, baking powder, and salt. Measure out the milk in a smaller bowl or measuring cup.

3. Swap out bowls from the stand mixer if you have extra bowls to spare, otherwise use a hand mixer. Beat the egg whites until stiff peaks are formed.

4. Swap bowls out again (if you just did so). With the motor running on medium speed, gradually alternate between adding the flour mixture and milk, starting and ending with the flour. Pause occasionally to scrape down the sides and bottom of the bowl. Once combined, stop the mixer.

5. Using a spatula, gently fold the egg whites and ⅔ cup (128g) sprinkles into the batter. Be sure to scrape sides and bottom of the bowl so all ingredients are well combined. Do not overmix. Evenly distribute the cake batter between the cake pans. Sprinkle the remaining 2 tablespoons (24g) sprinkles onto the top of the batter in the pans.

6. Bake for 35 to 40 minutes, or until a toothpick inserted in the center comes out clean (or with a few crumbs, but should not be wet). Cool in the pans on a cooling rack for 15 minutes. Then quickly flip the cakes onto the rack to invert and remove the pan. Allow to cool completely before frosting and decorating (page 120).

BABS SAYS...

This cake yields a good amount of batter, enough for 3 (8-inch/20cm) pans. If you do not want a 3-layer cake, you can divide the batter into 2 (9-inch/23cm) pans, and you'll have the perfect amount leftover to make a 2-layer smash cake with 4-inch (10cm) pans!

Do not use nonpareil (tiny ball-shaped) sprinkles because they will bleed. Only use traditional sprinkles, called jimmies.

Rotate the cake pans about halfway through to ensure even baking.

MAKE IT AHEAD

Freeze this cake for up to 3 months. Place in the freezer, uncovered, for 1 hour to set the frosting. Then wrap the cake in a double layer of plastic wrap, followed by aluminum foil. Thaw in the refrigerator the day before serving.

VANILLA BUTTERCREAM FROSTING

prep time
15 minutes

cook time
none

yield
enough for
1 (3-layer) round cake

This versatile buttercream recipe can be used as either a filling between cake layers or as a frosting to cover a cake. It's perfect on the Rainbow Sprinkle Funfetti Cake (page 119).

INGREDIENTS

1½ cups (336g) salted butter, softened

2lb (1kg) powdered sugar

2 tbsp pure vanilla extract or any extract flavoring of choice

⅓ cup + 1 tbsp whole milk, plus more if needed to thin

DIRECTIONS

1. In the bowl of a stand mixer fitted with the paddle attachment, cream the butter on medium speed for about 2 minutes, or until pale and fluffy.

2. Add the sugar. Mix on medium speed, pausing to scrape the bottom at least once or twice, until the mixture is clumpy. Reduce the speed and add the vanilla. Increase the speed to medium and mix until combined.

3. Reduce the speed and add the milk. Mix on medium speed for 30 seconds, or until the mixture is smooth.

4. Increase the speed to medium-high and whip for about 5 minutes, or until light and fluffy. Be sure to scrape the bottom and sides at least once. Adjust consistency with milk as desired. Use immediately, or refrigerate in an airtight container.

MAKE IT AHEAD
Make up to 3 days in advance. Store, tightly covered, in the refrigerator. When ready to use, allow to come to room temperature, and mix on medium-high until smooth.

SIMPLE LAYERED CAKE DECORATING

Cake layers, room temperature

Frosting

Decorations, such as sprinkles

1. Before icing the cake layers, be sure the cakes are completely cooled on both sides. They should not be warm to the touch.

2. Place a spoonful of frosting on the surface of the serving piece (cakeboard, serving platter, cake stand, etc.) you will be using, and spread it out so the first layer of cake sticks.

3. Place the first layer of cake onto the surface and gently press down to be sure it sticks to the frosting.

4. Rim the top perimeter of the cake with buttercream to create a border. You can do this with a piping bag if you have one, or by cutting a nickel-sized hole in the tip of a freezer zipper bag. Once you've created a border, you can add frosting to the center and spread with an offset spatula, smoothing as you go. You want to be sure the surface is even.

5. Add the next layer of cake and repeat the above steps for all layers. Once the top layer is complete, use the offset spatula to add the icing to the sides of the cake. Add sprinkles or other decorations, and voilà! Enjoy!

SMASH CAKE

I always look forward to our grandkids' first birthdays. My daughter loves showering her sons with smash cakes when they have that special birthday. She strips them down and lets them go at the cake! It's a ton of fun to see how their little personalities shine in this moment. This is not only the favorite of my one-year-old grandson Scooter, but also a hit with my toddler-aged grandkids, too. Even I love it! I've made this recipe as just a loaf when not celebrating a special one-year-old in the family. The cream cheese frosting and the cake are the perfect combo.

prep time
15 minutes, plus
2 hours to cool

cook time
50 minutes

yield
1 smash cake plus
1 loaf (serves
about 9)

MAKE IT AHEAD
Freeze for up to 3 months. Place in the freezer uncovered for 1 hour to set the frosting. Then wrap the cake in a double layer of plastic wrap, followed by aluminum foil. Thaw in the refrigerator the day before serving.

INGREDIENTS

½ cup (112g) unsalted butter, softened

½ cup (107g) firmly packed light brown sugar

2 large eggs

½ cup pure maple syrup

2 (4 oz/113g) containers unsweetened applesauce

1¾ cups (224g) all-purpose flour

2 tsp baking powder

1 tsp baking soda

½ tsp ground cinnamon

Pinch of fine kosher salt

Cream Cheese Frosting:

8 oz (226g) cream cheese, softened

½ cup (113g) unsalted butter, softened

2 cups (227g) powdered sugar

2 tsp pure vanilla extract

Natural food coloring (optional)

DIRECTIONS

1. Preheat the oven to 350°F (180°C). Grease and line 2 (4-inch/10cm) ramekins or cake pans, and 1 (9 x 5-inch/23 x 12.5cm) loaf pan with parchment paper.

2. In the bowl of a stand mixer fitted with the paddle attachment, beat the butter and sugar together until pale and creamy. Add the eggs one at a time, beating well after each addition. Add the maple syrup and applesauce. Beat until well combined.

3. Using a fine-mesh sieve, sift the flour, baking powder, baking soda, cinnamon, and salt into the wet mixture. Stir until combined. Spoon the mixture into the ramekins until three-fourths full. Pour the rest of the batter into the loaf pan.

4. Bake the smash cakes for 30 to 35 minutes, or until a toothpick inserted into the center comes out clean. Bake the loaf for an additional 15 minutes, or until a toothpick inserted in the center comes out clean. Let stand for 15 minutes before turning onto a wire rack to cool completely.

5. Make the frosting. In the bowl of a stand mixer fitted with the paddle attachment, beat the cream cheese and butter until well combined. Add the powdered sugar and vanilla. Beat until smooth and creamy, scraping the side of the bowl once or twice during mixing. If desired, beat in a few drops of natural food coloring of your choice.

6. To assemble the smash cake, place the bottom half on a serving plate. Spoon frosting over. Add the remaining layer. Spread frosting over the top and side of the cake. Add decorations of your choice. To serve the loaf, spread the top and sides with frosting, and cut into slices to serve.

PANCAKE BREAKFAST

prep time
15 minutes

cook time
15 minutes

yield
6

When my kids woke up on their birthday, the tradition in our family was to serve them breakfast in bed, even if it happened to fall on a school day. That breakfast was a hot stack of pancakes, the number coinciding with their birthday year, drizzled with warm maple syrup with candles on top. It was their first birthday "cake," kicking off a week of celebrations.

INGREDIENTS

1¼ cups (160g) all-purpose flour

1 tbsp baking powder

¼ tsp kosher salt

1 tbsp granulated sugar

1 large egg

2 cups whole milk

3 tbsp (42g) unsalted butter, melted

1 tsp pure vanilla extract

Toppings of choice

DIRECTIONS

1. In a medium bowl, whisk together the flour, baking powder, salt, and sugar.

2. In a separate medium bowl, beat the egg. Whisk in the milk, melted butter, and vanilla.

3. Pour the milk mixture into the dry ingredients. Whisk gently until just combined, being very careful not to overmix—small lumps are okay. Let the batter rest for 5 to 10 minutes

4. Meanwhile, get your favorite toppings ready. Preheat the griddle over medium heat, and lightly coat with nonstick spray.

5. When the griddle has been preheated and the batter rested, pour in ½-cup portions of batter. When bubbles appear on the surface, flip the pancakes.

6. Once they are flipped, sprinkle on those toppings. Cook for a few minutes more; be patient! Then stack your pancakes, and serve.

BABS SAYS...

You can swap out the whole milk with almond milk, buttermilk, or even coconut milk.

These freeze nicely if you have extras. Just place them in a freezer-safe bag. Pop into the microwave or oven when ready to serve.

Make 12 normal-sized pancakes using just 1½ cups milk and ¼-cup portions of batter.

TRADITIONS TO MAKE YOUR OWN

Host an annual outdoor potluck

Pick one day a week to eat a meal outside—
dinner at the park or your own backyard

Invest in some yard games; they always seem to bring
family and friends together

SUMMER
barbecue

We couldn't wait for summer to finally begin. At last, it was a time to have our kids all to ourselves with no schedules and no homework, just looking forward to the lazy days of summer. Now don't get me wrong. Summer also meant soccer camps, swim team, football camp, sleep away camp—yes, lots of activities, but at a different pace. It also meant spending endless hours outdoors. Even after dinner, the kids immediately headed back outside meeting the other neighborhood kids for a game of kick the can or ghost in the graveyard or a backyard camp out.

Summer also meant barbecues celebrating all the special holidays, starting with Memorial Day and the annual parade in which our own kids participated for so many years in the small town of Ridgefield, Connecticut. It was probably one of the few parades in the country you could see twice. Once the parade reached a certain intersection, the marchers made a U-turn and the parade continued back up Main Street, affording everyone an opportunity to see the parade twice—coming and going!

We celebrated not only all the patriotic holidays: 4th of July, Memorial Day, and Labor Day, but also other special events: Father's Day, National Hot Dog Day, block parties, picnics, and our annual road trip to Chicago to see our large extended family. During our visit each year, my Uncle Al celebrated his Fourth of July birthday with a pool party, along with Aunt Chickie's famous ribs. Aunt Chickie and Uncle Al had a beautiful pool in their backyard, and each summer many family parties were held there filled with yard games, music, and fun!

Summer was a time of celebration, and we used any excuse to get together with family, friends, and neighbors. The ease of a barbecue or picnic is that most recipes have to be prepared ahead of time to allow the flavors to meld or the meat to marinate before getting seared on a hot grill. Picnics and barbecues were made easy by using all the freshness of the fruits and vegetables that announced summer had finally arrived.

Our favorite summer refreshment is even a make-ahead drink, our Southern Slushies. Summer is the time for relaxing and enjoying the abundance of the season with family and friends in that casual, alfresco, party atmosphere we all love.

ON THE
TABLE

Broccoli Salad 129

Summer Fruit Salad
for a Crowd 131

Corn Salad 132

Hilda's Ranch Baked Beans . . . 135

Aunt Chickie's Famous Ribs . . . 137

Grilled Stuffed Flank Steak . . . 139

Lemon-Barbecued Chicken . . . 141

Fresh Peach Pie 143

Southern Slushies 145

BROCCOLI SALAD

This easy, crisp, classic vegetable salad is a must at any summer barbecue, picnic, or pool party. This is an old recipe I've been making for over forty years. The flavors meld beautifully, and the fresh crispness of the veggies, the creaminess of the dressing, and the ease of making it ahead, make this recipe a winner in all categories.

prep time
15 minutes, plus at least 1 hour to chill

cook time
none

serves
8–10

INGREDIENTS

2 bunches of raw broccoli, cut into bite-sized florets (about 8 cups)

1 small red onion, chopped

1 lb (450g) crisp, crumbled bacon

½ cup chopped, toasted pecans or walnuts

1 cup golden or brown raisins

1 cup mayonnaise

½ cup granulated sugar

2 tbsp apple cider vinegar

DIRECTIONS

1. In a large bowl, mix the broccoli, onion, bacon, nuts, and raisins.

2. In a small bowl, stir together the mayonnaise, sugar, and vinegar.

3. Toss the dressing with the broccoli mixture. Refrigerate for at least 1 hour before serving. Store leftovers in an airtight container in the refrigerator for up to 3 days.

BABS SAYS...
It really is important to allow the flavors of the salad to marry in the refrigerator before serving.

You could use ½ cup mayo and ½ cup sour cream, or even Greek yogurt, as a dressing alternative.

MAKE IT AHEAD
Prepare this salad up to 3 days in advance.

SUMMER FRUIT SALAD FOR A CROWD

I have made this delicious fruit salad more times than I can count. It was served at my cousin Pam's bridal shower, at many family picnics, and most recently at my daughter Elizabeth's baby shower. It serves a crowd, and with the brandy-infused peach sauce, this really is the most elegant fruit salad I have ever made.

prep time
40 minutes

cook time
none

serves
15–20

INGREDIENTS

1 large watermelon

1 cantaloupe or honeydew

2 pints (680g) strawberries, hulled and sliced

2 lb (1kg) fresh peaches, peeled and sliced

2 pints (680g) blueberries

Sauce:

1 lb (450g) peeled peaches

½ cup fresh lime juice

½ cup granulated sugar

¼ cup brandy

DIRECTIONS

1. In a food processor or blender, combine all of the ingredients for the sauce until smooth.

2. Use a melon baller to scoop the watermelon and cantaloupe into balls.

3. Add all of the fruit to a very large serving bowl, and toss gently in the sauce. Serve chilled or at room temperature.

BABS SAYS...

You can replace the brandy with any flavor of fruit juice.

You can serve the fruit salad in a large bowl, or you can use the empty watermelon rinds as your serving pieces.

MAKE IT AHEAD

Prepare all of the ingredients the night before, and assemble just before you serve.

CORN SALAD

prep time
15 minutes

cook time
15 minutes

serves
6–8

This salad has been served at many barbecues. The beauty is that it can be prepared in advance and tastes even better the longer the flavors marry. I have made it using the Cotija cheese, as well as the feta, and either one works beautifully. This salad is a springboard to wherever your creative juices lead you.

INGREDIENTS

6 ears fresh corn (shucked)

1½ tbsp olive oil

1 clove garlic, minced

1 cup cooked black beans, rinsed and drained

½ cup chopped cilantro leaves, plus more to garnish

1 red bell pepper, diced

1½ large avocados, diced

½ cup red onion, diced

½ cup Cotija or feta cheese, crumbled, plus more to garnish

Dressing:

1 tsp honey

1 tbsp fresh lime juice

½ tsp chili powder

¼ tsp ground cumin

¼ tsp kosher salt

½ cup mayonnaise

DIRECTIONS

1. Cut the fresh corn kernels from the cob. In a large sauté pan, sauté the oil and corn kernels over medium-high heat, stirring frequently, for 10 to 15 minutes, or until lightly charred. Add the minced garlic and cook for 1 minute more.

2. To a medium bowl, add the charred corn and garlic, the black beans, cilantro, bell pepper, avocados, red onion, and cheese. Toss gently.

3. In a small bowl, whisk together all of the ingredients for the dressing. Pour over the salad, and toss gently to coat. Finish off with a sprinkling of additional cheese and cilantro.

4. Serve chilled or at room temperature. Store leftovers in an airtight container in the refrigerator for up to 4 days.

BABS SAYS...

This versatile recipe can be served as a dip, as well as a side dish to grilled meat, fish or your favorite Tex-Mex dishes.

If you'd like to serve this as a warm side dish, combine everything in the bowl except the charred corn mixture. When ready to serve, cook the corn and toss it in the salad hot.

MAKE IT AHEAD

Prepare this salad up to 2 days in advance, reserving the avocado until ready to serve. Just toss gently before serving, and garnish with some fresh cilantro and cheese, plus the avocado.

HILDA'S RANCH BAKED BEANS

prep time
5 minutes

cook time
40 minutes

serves
6

Hilda was our next-door neighbor in Virginia. We shared a lot of laughs and some of our favorite recipes. Before tasting Hilda's version, I used to soak raw beans overnight and then slow cook them for hours to make baked beans. Then I tasted Hilda's rendition, which was a lot easier and just as delicious. This is a stovetop-to-oven recipe that can be prepared ahead of time and the perfect dish to take to your next neighborhood barbecue or picnic. It scales easily, so make as much as you want.

INGREDIENTS

6 slices bacon

1 large onion, thinly sliced

1 clove garlic, crushed

½ cup thinly sliced green bell pepper

1 (28 oz/800g) can pork and beans, such as B&M Baked Beans

½ cup barbecue sauce, such as Sweet Baby Ray's Original

2 tbsp molasses or honey

DIRECTIONS

1. Preheat the oven to 350°F (180°C). In a large sauté pan, cook the bacon over medium-low heat until almost crispy. Remove and drain the bacon. Reserve 3 tablespoons rendered fat in the skillet.

2. Add the onion, garlic, and pepper. Cook over medium heat for 5 to 7 minutes, or until tender. Add the beans, barbecue sauce, and molasses, and thoroughly combine.

3. Pour the ingredients into a 1.5-quart (1.5L) casserole dish. Crumble the bacon and sprinkle over top. Bake, uncovered, for 30 minutes, and serve.

MAKE IT AHEAD

Prepare this up to 3 days in advance, and store, covered, in the refrigerator. To reheat, cover tightly with aluminum foil and put in the oven at 350°F (180°C) for about 20 minutes.

You can also freeze them. Spoon the beans into a reusable freezer bag or airtight container, seal tightly, and freeze for up to 9 months.

AUNT CHICKIE'S FAMOUS RIBS

Summers spent in Oakbrook, Illinois, at Aunt Chickie and Uncle Al's house meant family, fun, swimming, and food—lots of food. One of our favorites was my aunt's amazing barbecued ribs. These were a seasonal favorite, but since most of the tenderizing takes place in a low-temp oven, they are something that can be enjoyed all year long. With a recipe this easy, there are no excuses for not including them on your barbecue table. Aunt Chickie put cinnamon in her rub, and we never looked back.

prep time
10 minutes, plus 3 hours or overnight to marinate

cook time
3 hours

serves
6

INGREDIENTS

2 racks baby back pork ribs (12 bones; about 1½ lbs/680g each)

2 lemons, juiced

Barbecue sauce, such as Sweet Baby Ray's Honey, to coat

Rub:

2 tbsp kosher salt

1 tbsp light brown sugar

1 tbsp sweet paprika

1 tbsp chili powder

1 tbsp garlic powder

1 tbsp onion powder

1 tsp freshly ground black pepper

1 tsp white pepper

1 tsp ground cinnamon

½ tsp cayenne

DIRECTIONS

1. To make the rub, combine all of the ingredients in a small bowl.

2. Prep the ribs. Remove the shiny silver membrane on the concave side of the ribs by slipping a paring knife under one end of the membrane. Move the knife back and forth so you are able to get a few fingers under the membrane. Grab the membrane with a paper towel and remove. Remove any excess fat from the ribs.

3. Rub the ribs all over with lemon juice. Coat the ribs thoroughly with the dry rub mixture. Tightly wrap them in plastic wrap. Refrigerate for at least 3 hours or overnight.

4. When ready to cook, preheat the oven to 300°F (150°C) with the rack in the middle of the oven. Line a large baking pan with foil. Place the ribs meat-side down in the pan, and cover tightly with foil. Bake for 2 hours 30 minutes.

5. Preheat the grill. Remove the pan from the oven and pour off the liquid. Brush barbecue sauce all over the ribs.

6. Remove the ribs from the pan and place directly on the grill grates, turning and basting with additional barbecue sauce, for 10 minutes. Serve immediately.

BABS SAYS...

You can ask your butcher to remove the membrane from the ribs, which will save you some time.

If you don't have a grill, these can be finished off in the oven. Set the oven to broil. Return the ribs to the middle rack, basting and broiling for about 5 minutes per side.

MAKE IT AHEAD

Store the cooked ribs through step 4 in the refrigerator for up to 1 day. Let them come to room temperature and sear before serving.

GRILLED STUFFED FLANK STEAK

This is a recipe that takes flank steak to the next level. Marinating the steak packs it with flavor while tenderizing this reasonably priced cut of meat. We were able to serve steak to four kids without breaking the budget. However, the finished product is delicious enough to serve at a high-end restaurant.

prep time
20 minutes, plus overnight to marinate

cook time
15 minutes

serves
8 (2 pinwheels per serving)

INGREDIENTS

2 beef flank steaks (1½ lb/680g each)

1 tsp garlic salt

½ tsp freshly ground black pepper

2 tbsp Pecorino Romano cheese

½ lb (225g) bacon slices, cooked until almost crispy

1 cup fresh baby spinach

Marinade:

½ cup olive oil

¼ cup soy sauce

3 tbsp honey

2 tbsp apple cider vinegar

1½ tsp ground ginger

2 cloves garlic, chopped

DIRECTIONS

1. Prepare the marinade. In a small bowl, whisk together all of the ingredients until thoroughly combined.

2. Pound the steaks to an even thickness, about ½ inch (1.25cm) thick. Score one side of the flank steaks in a crosshatch pattern. Add the steaks to a resealable zipper bag, along with the marinade. Refrigerate overnight.

3. When ready to cook, preheat the grill to medium. Lay the steaks flat on a surface, scored-side down. Evenly sprinkle them with the garlic salt, pepper, and Pecorino Romano, and evenly arrange the spinach. Lay the strips of bacon horizontally over the seasoned steaks.

4. Roll up the steaks in jelly-roll fashion, starting at the narrow edge. Skewer each steak with 8 long, wooden toothpicks at 1-inch (2.5cm) intervals. With a serrated knife, cut each rolled steak into 8 (1-inch/2.5cm) rounds.

5. Grill the rounds for 10 to 15 minutes, turning once, until cooked as desired. Serve immediately.

BABS SAYS...
You can vary the stuffing to whatever sounds great. I have used basil pesto instead of spinach, and that's delicious, too!

MAKE IT AHEAD
Fully assemble and slice the stuffed steak up to 2 days in advance, stored tightly covered in the refrigerator. Take them out of the refrigerator 30 minutes before grilling.

LEMON-BARBECUED CHICKEN

prep time
10 minutes,
plus overnight
to marinate

cook time
35 minutes

serves
8

When we moved from Chicago with our two little sons, far from family and life-long friends, we all experienced a sense of loss. However, moving to a beautiful place called Brandermill eased this transition. This planned community made making new friends so easy. We had progressive dinners, an active church community, and loads of activities for the kids. The dinners gave Bill and me a chance to savor good food and enjoy our new friends who heralded from many different states and even countries. This recipe was served at a summer picnic event—a fresh, rich, lemon chicken that is marinated the night before grilling.

INGREDIENTS

2 chickens, cut up into
  bone-in pieces
  (see Babs Says…)

Marinade:
2 tsp onion powder
2 tsp dried basil, crushed
½ tsp ground thyme
½ tsp garlic powder
1 cup olive or avocado oil
½ cup lemon juice
1 tbsp kosher salt
1 tsp sweet paprika

DIRECTIONS

1. In a small bowl, whisk together all of the ingredients for the marinade. Place the chicken pieces in a resealable plastic bag or large bowl, and pour the marinade over the chicken. Cover tightly and refrigerate for 8 hours or overnight, turning occasionally.

2. Grease the grates of the grill and preheat to 400°F (200°C) (see Babs Says…). Once preheated, lower the temperature to 350°F (180°C). Place the chicken on the grates, reserving the marinade for basting, and close the lid. Grill on one side for 7 minutes, or until the chicken naturally releases from the grates. Once the chicken easily releases, flip and baste the chicken. Grill for another 7 minutes. Once the chicken releases easily again, move all the pieces to one side of the grill and baste.

3. Turn off the burners directly under the chicken while leaving the other burners on to maintain indirect heat. Close the lid and cook the chicken for 10 minutes. Baste the chicken and close the lid for another 10 minutes, or until the chicken pieces reach an internal temperature of 165°F (75°C). Enjoy immediately.

BABS SAYS…
Often you can buy whole chickens cut up into pieces (legs, breasts, thighs, wings). You can ask the butcher to cut it, also. If you like dark meat, then stick with just legs and thighs.

While the grill is still cold, grease the grates with a paper towel that has been dipped in olive or avocado oil. This will prevent your food from sticking.

FRESH PEACH PIE

During the summer months, retrieving fresh fruit from Silverman's Farm was on the calendar for at least three visits. At the height of peach-picking season, we would take care to choose the perfect fruit because nothing tastes like summer more than a juicy, ripe peach. Peach pie was always on the menu after our visit. This is a scrumptious way to use those sweet summer peaches. This recipe uses a single, flaky pie crust to hold the peach filling and is topped with a sweet streusel topping. What could be better?

prep time
30 minutes, plus
1 hour to chill and set

cook time
50 minutes

serves
8

INGREDIENTS

Vanilla ice cream or heavy cream, to serve

Crust:
1¼ cups (160g) all-purpose flour
¼ cup (29g) powdered sugar
Pinch of kosher salt
½ cup (112g) unsalted butter, cold, cut into small pieces
2 large egg yolks
1 tbsp ice-cold water (approximately)

Filling:
2 lbs (1kg) ripe peaches (about 6)
⅓ cup (67g) granulated sugar
¼ cup (32g) all-purpose flour
1 tbsp fresh lemon juice

Streusel topping:
½ cup (100g) granulated sugar
½ cup (64g) all-purpose flour
⅓ cup (75g) unsalted butter, softened

DIRECTIONS

1. Grease a 9-inch (23cm) pie dish. Prepare the crust. In a medium bowl, whisk together the flour, sugar, and salt. Cut in the butter until well combined and the mixture resembles coarse sand. Add the egg yolks and just enough ice-cold water to mix to a soft dough.

2. Turn the dough out onto a lightly floured surface. Press the mixture together to form a disc. Wrap in plastic wrap and chill for 30 minutes.

3. Roll the pastry out on a lightly floured surface until large enough to fit the pie dish. Line the pie dish with the pastry. Trim and crimp the edge.

4. Preheat the oven to 375°F (190°C) with the rack on the bottom. Make the filling. Fill a large pot with water and bring to a boil. With a knife, score the peaches on the bottom, making a small X. Prepare an ice water bath. Add the peaches to the boiling water for 1 minute. Immediately remove and place in the ice-water bath to cool. Once cool, peel the skins off with a paring knife. Cut the peaches into slices and place in a large bowl. Add the sugar, flour, and lemon juice. Toss to combine.

5. Make the streusel topping. In a medium bowl, combine the sugar and flour. With a pastry blender, a fork, or clean hands, work the softened butter into the mixture until coarse crumbs form.

6. Fill the pie crust with the peach filling. Sprinkle the streusel over the peach filling. Bake on the bottom rack for 50 minutes, or until the crust is golden. Let stand for at least 30 minutes before cutting into wedges. Serve with ice cream or heavy cream.

BABS SAYS...
I only use fresh peaches for this pie since I only make it during the summer peach season. However, you could use frozen peaches, thawed and drained of liquid.

Okay, you're busy. If you don't have the time, buy a ready-made crust, no judgment here! It's all about the filling, anyway.

MAKE IT AHEAD
Fully prepare and cook the pie up to 3 days ahead of time, stored tightly covered in the refrigerator. Reheat in the oven at 300°F (150°C) until warm.

SOUTHERN SLUSHIES

prep time
30 minutes, plus
3 days to freeze

cook time
10 minutes

serves
20

My friend Susie gave me this fabulous drink concoction way back in the 1970s, and it's been one of our go-to summer drinks ever since. The tropical-flavored ice crystals topped off with the lemon-lime carbonated soda immediately quenches any summer thirst. These are so easy to throw together, and you literally have drinks for a crowd at the ready when needed. By the way, we have enjoyed these in other seasons, as well!

INGREDIENTS

7 cups water, divided

1½ cups granulated sugar

3 black tea bags

1 (12 fl oz/355ml) can frozen lemonade

1 (12 fl oz/355ml) can frozen orange juice

3 cups brandy (see Babs Says...)

Lemon-lime soda, such as 7Up or Sprite, to cover

Orange twists, to garnish

DIRECTIONS

1. In a large pot, boil 5 cups water, along with the granulated sugar, for 2 minutes. Let cool.

2. In a small pot, boil the remaining 2 cups water and add the tea bags. Steep until dark. Let cool.

3. To the large pot of cooled sugar water, add the cooled tea mixture, frozen lemonade, frozen orange juice, and brandy. Mix thoroughly. Freeze in an airtight container for at least 3 days before serving.

4. For each serving, fill a glass about two-thirds full with the slush mixture, fluff with a fork, and top off the last one-third of the glass with the lemon-lime soda. Garnish with a twist of orange, and enjoy!

BABS SAYS...

Use a very reasonably priced (60 proof or less) brandy...no reason to go top shelf here. For an added twist, try using flavored brandy.

MAKE IT AHEAD

You need to make this one at least 3 days in advance because it takes a long time for the mixture to become fairly frozen because of the alcohol and sugar content.

You can also divide the mixture into smaller portions to freeze so you always have the right amount on hand.

TRADITIONS TO MAKE YOUR OWN

Sport dirndls and lederhosen and find a nearby
German fest

Use Oktoberfest as a theme for a dinner or party
any time of year, such as a back-to-school block party

Organize a German beer tasting—remember to say *prost!*

OKTOBERFEST
party

My first exposure to Oktoberfest was when I attended college in Milwaukee, a very German city. Oktoberfest was all about music, brats, and beer. The fun all took place in Heidelberg Park at the Bavarian Bierhaus.

Years later, we tried to recapture those days with our annual Bobby's Court Oktoberfest Block Party. This was the last outdoor party of the season. The party was held on a cul-de-sac where the kids could ride their big wheels while the older kids and adults gathered to try their skill at a basketball competition and a volleyball game. Events were planned for the kids, including a water balloon toss, an egg throwing contest, face painting, and a potato sack race, among other fun activities.

However, the main attraction was the food. From beer marinated brats to German roasted potato salad and Grandma Soden's German cheesecake, the theme was pure Oktoberfest. Did I mention the keg of beer that was ice cold and on tap? Well, that was enjoyed by all.

After my daughter gave birth to her first born, Charlie, an Oktoberfest first birthday party was planned. People came from near and far to celebrate this precious little one's first year of life. Charlie even wore a onesie lederhosen. The party was held on the rooftop of their apartment building. There was a large barbecue grill and an entertainment area. We once again served the marinated brats, but this time with a new twist on the toppings that were loved by all: a brat right off the grill placed in a brioche bun, thinly sliced cucumber tucked into the sides, some pickled daikon and carrot layered on top, sriracha aioli drizzled over, and four slices of fresh jalapeño placed along the top. My nephew Joe's famous beer cheese and homemade pretzels were a huge hit, followed by a lederhosen-decorated smash cake. It ended up being the perfect theme for a fall first birthday.

In so many ways, Oktoberfest is the celebration signaling the end of summer and the beginning of fall, a celebration that now has a special family connection—our grandson's birthday.

ON THE
TABLE

Creamy Beer Cheese Dip 151

Brats & All the Trimmings 152

Sriracha Aioli 154

Pickled Carrots & Daikon 154

Soft Pretzels 155

German Roasted
Potato Salad 157

Grandma Soden's German
Cheesecake 159

CREAMY BEER CHEESE DIP

prep time
10 minutes

cook time
15 minutes

yield
2 cups

My nephew Joe is one of the family's "beer sommeliers." He and my other nephew, Alex, know beer and all things related to beer. This is Joe's famous German beer dip because he not only knows all things beer, but he also knows all things German.

INGREDIENTS

3 tbsp unsalted butter

3 tbsp all-purpose flour

¾ cup dark lager, room temperature

¾ cup whole milk, room temperature

1 tsp Dijon mustard

¼ tsp garlic powder

¼ tsp kosher salt

⅛ tsp paprika

1½ cups freshly grated Gruyère cheese

1½ cups freshly grated extra-sharp cheddar cheese

Soft pretzels (page 155), tortilla chips, veggies, apples, pears, brats, nachos, hot dogs, etc., to serve

DIRECTIONS

1. In a medium saucepan, melt the butter over medium-low heat. Whisk in the flour to make a roux, cooking for 30 seconds while constantly whisking.

2. Continue whisking while slowly pouring in the dark lager. Simmer for about 3 minutes, whisking constantly.

3. While whisking continuously, slowly pour in the milk. Simmer for about 3 minutes, whisking constantly.

4. Whisk in the Dijon, garlic powder, salt, and paprika. Remove from the heat.

5. Stir in the shredded cheeses about 1 cup at a time. Continue adding the cheese and whisking until thickened, creamy, and smooth.

6. Pour the dip in a 1-quart (1L) bowl. Serve immediately with soft pretzels, chips, tortillas, veggies, apples, pears, brats, nachos, hot dogs... you get the picture!

BABS SAYS...

You can use any type of beer, however, the dark lager enhances the depth of flavor. You can choose not to use the beer and substitute an additional ¾ cup milk.

MAKE IT AHEAD

Make the dip 2 to 3 weeks in advance. Store in an airtight container in the refrigerator. Reheat in the microwave; on the stovetop over low heat, stirring occasionally; or in a slow cooker, set to warm, for about 1 hour.

Yes, the creamy beer dip can be frozen. Just add a touch of heavy cream to the dip, and combine. Store in an airtight container or freezer-safe bag, making sure not to fill the bag to the top because the mixture will expand.

BRATS & ALL
THE TRIMMINGS

There's nothing like a bratwurst soaked in beer and then grilled to perfection. In fact, I have been making these Oktoberfest staples for many years, including at numerous neighborhood block parties. These mouthwatering sausages, topped with all the accoutrements, on a beer-moistened roll, make the Oktoberfest season beautiful and delicious. We serve the brats two ways: traditional and with an unexpected twist.

prep time
5 minutes

cook time
30 minutes

serves
10

INGREDIENTS

2 cups pilsner or lager

2 cups cold water

2 medium onions, chopped

10 bratwursts

10 brioche hot dog rolls

Unexpected Trimmings:

Pickled Carrots & Daikon
(page 154)

Cucumbers, thinly sliced
lengthwise

Sriracha Aioli (page 154)

Cilantro

Jalapeños, seeded and
thinly sliced

Traditional Trimmings:

Mustard

Beer-soaked onions

DIRECTIONS

1. In a large pot, add the pilsner, water, and onions. Bring to a boil over high heat, and then immediately turn down the heat to keep the liquid at a simmer. Add the bratwurst. Slowly simmer the brats for 10 minutes, making sure not to boil them so the casings don't split. After 10 minutes, remove the brats. While simmering the brats, preheat the grill and grease the grates.

2. Continue simmering the onions for another 10 minutes, or until the beer is reduced. Reserve the beer-soaked onions for topping the brats.

3. Grill the simmered brats over medium heat until all sides are golden brown, about 10 minutes.

4. Serve immediately on buns with the unexpected trimmings (in the order listed) or the traditional trimmings.

BABS SAYS...

You have to avoid splitting the brat casings at all costs—that would be a certain way to ruin a juicy, succulent sausage!

The brats can be made ahead of time and kept warm. After grilling, move the brats to the unheated or cooler side of the grill. With the lid closed, the brats will keep warm without overcooking. Another way of keeping the brats warm is to store them in a beer bath. Fill an aluminum pan with warm beer and place on the cooler side of the grill. Close the lid, and when ready, serve directly from the pan.

SRIRACHA AIOLI

prep time
5 minutes

cook time
none

serves
10

For my grandson's Oktoberfest birthday party, my daughter and I decided to take it up a notch. Many years ago, Liz discovered a small German food joint in Manhattan, famous for its unique toppings for its bratwurst. We served these Asian–inspired brats with sriracha aioli and pickled carrots and daikon, and they were the hit of the party.

INGREDIENTS	DIRECTIONS
2 cups mayonnaise	1. Thoroughly combine all ingredients. Transfer the sauce to a squeeze bottle to easily dispense. (It's also great on burgers!) Store in an airtight container in the refrigerator for up to 1 week.
½ cup sriracha	
4 cloves garlic, grated	
1½ tbsp pickle juice	
1 tsp paprika	
Salt, to taste	
Freshly ground black pepper, to taste	

PICKLED CARROTS & DAIKON

prep time
15 minutes, plus at least
2 days to pickle

cook time
1 hour

serves
10

INGREDIENTS	DIRECTIONS
½ cup granulated sugar	1. In a medium saucepan, combine the sugar, salt, water, vinegar, and pepper. Bring to a boil, and then add the vegetable shreds. Simmer for 1 hour.
1 tbsp salt	
½ cup water	2. Pour the liquid and vegetables into a jar, making sure the veggies are submerged.
½ cup white vinegar	
1 tsp freshly ground black pepper	3. Screw on the lid, and refrigerate to pickle for at least 2 days before using...waiting longer before serving is even better. These will keep for a very long time if kept submerged in the liquid.
8 oz (225g) daikon radishes, peeled and grated into thick shreds	
8 oz (225g) carrots, peeled and grated into thick shreds	

SOFT PRETZELS

prep time
20 minutes

cook time
15 minutes

yield
6

My dear friend Betsy shared this recipe so long ago when we taught preschool together. For years, the children at the Growing Tree Nursery School enjoyed rolling the dough and customizing their pretzels. They are that easy to make, and nothing beats a soft pretzel dipped in beer cheese—especially not a homemade one.

MAKE IT AHEAD
Cover and store pretzels at room temperature for up to 3 days.

INGREDIENTS

1 (¼ oz/2¼ tsp) pkg instant dry yeast

1 scant tbsp granulated sugar

1 qt (1L) + ¾ cup warm water (about 100°F/ 38°C), divided

2 cups (256g) all-purpose flour

½ tsp kosher salt

¼ cup (72g) baking soda

Toppings of choice, such as coarse salt, cinnamon-sugar, sesame seeds, poppy seeds, caraway seeds, everything mix, melted butter, etc.

DIRECTIONS

1. In a small bowl, dissolve the yeast and sugar in ¾ cup warm water. Let sit until bubbly, about 10 minutes.

2. Preheat the oven to 425°F (220°C). Add the flour and salt to the bowl of a food processor. Pulse a few times to combine.

3. With the processor running, slowly pour in the yeast mixture through the feed tube. Process until the dough comes together. If too moist, add more flour a teaspoon at a time.

4. Remove from the processor and turn onto a lightly floured surface. Knead a few times.

5. In a large skillet, dissolve the baking soda into the remaining 1 quart (1L) water. Heat slowly over medium heat until simmering.

6. Divide the dough evenly into 6 pieces. Roll each piece into an 18- to 24-inch (46–61cm) rope. To shape each pretzel, place the rope in a U-shape. Cross the two ends at the top. Fold the cross down, and press to make a pretzel shape.

7. Submerge the pretzels one at a time into the water mixture for 30 seconds, flipping once halfway through. Place onto a greased baking sheet.

8. While the pretzels are wet, sprinkle or brush with the toppings of your choice. Bake for 15 minutes, or until golden brown. Serve immediately.

GERMAN ROASTED POTATO SALAD

prep time
10 minutes

cook time
30 minutes

serves
6–8

I went to school in Milwaukee, home to some of the best German food in the country. Did I also mention it is considered the beer capital of the world? More importantly, I met so many wonderful people during those years, many of German descent, who are still dear friends to this day. However, 175 miles from Milwaukee is where the Oktoberfest to end all other celebrations takes place, and that's in the city of La Crosse, Wisconsin. German beer and food are everywhere. This recipe is a roasted version of the famous Bavarian salad.

INGREDIENTS

3 lbs (1.5kg) red potatoes, scrubbed, cut into 2in (5cm) chunks

3 tbsp extra-virgin olive oil

Sea salt, to season

Freshly ground black pepper, to season

8 strips uncooked bacon

1 medium onion, finely chopped

½ cup white vinegar

½ cup water

1 tbsp granulated sugar

1 tbsp whole-grain German mustard

¼ cup chopped parsley

DIRECTIONS

1. Preheat the oven to 425°F (220°C) with the rack in the middle of the oven. Line a baking sheet with foil, and lightly grease with nonstick cooking spray. Toss the potatoes with the oil, and season generously with salt and pepper. Arrange the potatoes in a single layer on the baking sheet. Make sure not to crowd the potatoes, or else they'll steam—use 2 baking sheets if you need to.

2. Place the baking sheet on the middle rack. Roast until the potatoes are golden brown on the outside and creamy in the middle, 25 to 35 minutes. Transfer to a large bowl and set aside.

3. While the potatoes are roasting, in a large skillet, fry the bacon over medium heat until crispy. Transfer the bacon to a paper towel–lined plate to drain, and then crumble. Discard all but ¼ cup bacon fat from the skillet.

4. Return the skillet with the bacon fat to medium heat, and add the onion. Cook until softened and just beginning to brown.

5. Stir in the vinegar, water, and sugar. Increase the heat to high. Bring to a boil, and reduce the liquid to ¾ cup, about 5 minutes or so. Remove the skillet from the heat.

6. Whisk in the mustard. Pour the mixture over the warm potatoes. Sprinkle the crumbled bacon over top, and garnish with chopped parsley. Taste and adjust the seasoning. Serve warm or at room temperature.

BABS SAYS...

Make certain to use whole-grain mustard.

Making this salad early in the day allows the flavors to marry. You can serve it at room temperature as well as warm.

MAKE IT AHEAD

Make this up to 1 week in advance. Just give the salad a good stir to reincorporate the ingredients.

GRANDMA SODEN'S GERMAN CHEESECAKE

Some friends are lifelong. My friend Sandy is one of those. We date back to freshman year in high school. Her grandma was a delight. I remember her vats of cucumbers in her pantry marinating in their pickling juice, and Saturday mornings taking her "class" on making yeast dough. But my absolute favorite recipe was her German cheesecake. She sprinkled raisins in her batter before baking. I make it more kid-friendly and substitute with mini chocolate chips.

prep time
30 minutes, plus
2 hours to cool
and chill

cook time
1 hour

serves
6–8

INGREDIENTS

Crust:

1¼ cups (125g) graham cracker crumbs

¼ cup (50g) granulated sugar

¼ cup (56g) salted butter, melted

Filling:

1 lb (450g) large-curd cottage cheese

1 lb (450g) cream cheese, room temperature

1 cup (227g) sour cream, room temperature

1 cup (200g) granulated sugar

5 large eggs, room temperature

1 tsp pure vanilla extract

Juice from ½ large lemon

Two handfuls raisins or mini chocolate chips, divided

Topping:

1 cup (227g) sour cream

3 heaped tbsp (40g) granulated sugar

½ cup (60g) chopped, toasted pecans

DIRECTIONS

1. Prepare the crust. In a medium bowl, combine all of the ingredients. Press into a 9- or 10-inch (23 or 25cm) springform pan. Refrigerate.

2. Prepare the filling. Into a medium bowl, press the cottage cheese through a sieve with the back of a spoon.

3. In a large bowl, beat the cream cheese and sour cream until well blended. Gradually beat in the sugar. Add the cottage cheese, and mix well. Add the eggs, one at a time, beating well after each addition. Stir in the vanilla and the lemon juice.

4. Preheat the oven to 350°F (180°C). Remove the crust from the refrigerator and sprinkle 1 handful of raisins or chocolate chips on the cheesecake crust. Pour half of the filling in the pan, and sprinkle with the remaining handful of raisins or chocolate chips. Add the rest of the filling. Bake for 1 hour. Cool for 15 minutes in the pan.

5. For the topping, combine the sour cream and sugar. Spread on the partially cooled cheesecake, and top with the pecans.

6. Let cool for 1 hour more on the counter in the pan, and then refrigerate for 1 hour. Once chilled, remove the cake from the springform pan. Slice and serve. The cheesecake is best enjoyed at room temperature.

MAKE IT AHEAD

Make this up to 4 days in advance. Cover tightly with plastic wrap and refrigerate.

If storing longer than a few days, the cheesecake should be frozen. To freeze, wrap the cheesecake in plastic wrap and place in an airtight container. When sealed this way, it will last for 2 to 3 months. You could also slice it in individual servings and freeze the same way.

When ready to serve, take the cake out of the freezer the night before and thaw in the refrigerator. If you need to thaw quickly, unwrap the frozen cake, and keep it on the counter to thaw for about 2 hours.

TRADITIONS TO MAKE YOUR OWN

Make New Pond Farm Chili (page 165) each year
before you go trick or treating

Visit a pumpkin patch, carve pumpkins, and clean an
extra one as a cauldron for root beer floats

Watch some scary—or not so scary—movies in the
week leading up to Halloween

HALLOWEEN
festivities

As a preschool teacher, October was a special and very busy month. We kicked off the month with our annual field trip to Warrup's Farm, including pumpkin picking, a corn maze, and a hayride. Our Halloween party at the end of the month was a family event that everyone enjoyed. The tradition of making witch's brew, something I had done for my own kids and passed on to my preschoolers, was always a hit. I would hollow out a pumpkin and call it a cauldron. I then would fill the cauldron with vanilla ice cream and fill a clear pitcher with root beer. I wore a witch's hat, and as the class was singing the *Stirring the Brew* song, I slowly poured the dark mixture into the pumpkin. As it hit the ice cream, the root beer foamed. When we finally all sang the last few words of the song, the brew was ready to be served. I still remember the surprise on those little cherub faces when the brave ones who were willing to try it took their first sip. Root beer floats never tasted so good!

For my own children, going to Blue Jay Orchards for their haunted house and haunted hayride was always an event the kids couldn't wait for. That being said, after a long wait in line, when it was our turn to enter the house, even the parents hung back a bit.

Because our neighborhood was filled with kids, the plans had already been set as to who was trick or treating with whom. For the younger set, the dads would accompany the little ones so the moms could stay home to pass out the candy. The older ones stayed in the neighborhood, and with people everywhere and lights ablaze, they made their way trying to cover as many houses as possible before their curfew. Years later, there was even a truck filled with hay that was provided by a local family. The kids could literally hop off and on the hayride as it continually made its way around the neighborhood.

Our tradition was to have a simple dinner ready to go before the costumes were donned. A pot of chili and some corn pudding were quickly eaten as the sun set because the trick or treating was about to begin! Now we enjoy seeing all the grandkids continue the tradition of celebrating Halloween.

ON THE
TABLE

New Pond Farm Chili 165

Corn Pudding. 167

Baked Caramel Corn 168

Taffy Apple Salad 171

Mrs. Williams's
Peanut Butter Bars 173

Ellen's Pumpkin Loaf. 175

Mulled Apple Cider 177

NEW POND FARM CHILI

New Pond Farm and I go way back to my days as a preschool teacher with the Growing Tree Nursery School. Each year, our children spent two glorious days at this quintessential New England farm making apple cider, participating in farm chores, and catching salamanders. During their seasonal festivals, the farm was filled with excited children and their families, enjoying sheep shearing, dancing around the Maypole, and feasting on delicious fare, which included their New Pond Farm Chili. This has been a recipe we have enjoyed throughout the years and is now a favorite of my grandson Charlie, with whom I visit New Pond Farm, but now as a grandmother!

prep time
15 minutes

cook time
1 hour 15 minutes

serves
a lot!

INGREDIENTS

⅓ cup olive oil

2 onions, chopped

1 red bell pepper, chopped

2 cloves garlic, minced

3 tbsp chili powder

1 tbsp ground cumin

¾ tsp dried oregano

1½ tbsp dried basil

½ tbsp garlic powder

½ tbsp salt

¾ tsp freshly ground black pepper

½ tsp crushed red pepper (or to taste)

2½ lb (1.25kg) ground beef

1 lb (450g) sweet Italian sausage (casings removed)

1 (28 oz/800g) can whole tomatoes and their juice (undrained)

1 (28 oz/800g) can tomato purée

2 lb (1kg) canned kidney beans, rinsed and drained

1 whole cinnamon stick

Shredded cheese, sour cream, green onions, and avocado, to serve

DIRECTIONS

1. In a Dutch oven, heat the olive oil over medium heat. Sauté the onions, bell pepper, and garlic for 5 to 7 minutes until soft, stirring occasionally. Stir in all of the spices and cook for a few minutes.

2. To the Dutch oven, add the ground beef a little at a time, stirring and browning, until all the meat is added and browned. Repeat with the sausage.

3. Crush the whole tomatoes with your hands, and add this to the Dutch oven. Add the tomato purée and the kidney beans. Add the cinnamon stick. Mix everything together and simmer for 1 hour. Remove the cinnamon stick.

4. Garnish with the desired toppings, and serve.

BABS SAYS...
Have you ever tried crushed pineapple with your chili? It's delicious!

MAKE IT AHEAD
Prepare this up to 5 days in advance, storing, covered, in the refrigerator. You can also freeze this in an airtight container for up to 3 months. Thaw in the refrigerator the day before serving, or defrost it in the microwave.

CORN PUDDING

prep time
5 minutes

cook time
1 hour

serves
8

Think of marriage between pudding and cake—that's corn pudding. It's a perfect accompaniment to chili, baked ham, barbecued ribs, or brisket. Corn pudding is one of those dishes that's a must next to chili, and never misses a spot on our Thanksgiving menu. However, this recipe is so versatile, easy, and delicious that it can be enjoyed throughout the year.

INGREDIENTS

1 (15 oz/420g) can whole kernel corn

1 (15 oz/420g) can cream-style sweet corn

½ cup unsalted butter, melted

1 cup sour cream

1 (8.5 oz/240g) box cornbread mix, such as Jiffy

3 large eggs, well beaten

½ tsp kosher salt

DIRECTIONS

1. Preheat the oven to 350°F (180°C). Grease a 9-inch (23cm) square pan.

2. In a large bowl, thoroughly mix together all of the ingredients. Pour into the pan. Bake for 45 minutes to 1 hour, or until browned.

3. Slice or scoop, and serve hot.

BABS SAYS...
For a Tex-Mex flare, add a 4-ounce (110g) can of green chiles, drained, and ½ cup grated cheddar cheese.

MAKE IT AHEAD
Prepare this up to 2 days in advance, and store, tightly covered, in the refrigerator. When ready to serve, let the corn pudding come to room temperature. Cover with foil, and place in a preheated 300°F (150°C) oven for 15 to 20 minutes, or until heated through.

The corn pudding can also be frozen for up to 3 months.

BAKED CARAMEL CORN

When I was growing up in Chicago, Cracker Jack popcorn was one of my favorite treats. The caramel corn and nuts were the ultimate snack, and the tiny toy hidden in the box only made Cracker Jack all that more appealing. Now you can make this quintessential all-American snack right in your own home for your little trick-or-treaters. This is an easy recipe that you can throw together in no time, so put on your favorite scary Halloween movie and enjoy!

prep time
5 minutes,
plus cooling

cook time
35 minutes

yield
9 cups

INGREDIENTS

12 cups (3 qt) freshly popped popcorn

½ cup chopped pecans

½ cup butter or margarine

1 cup firmly packed brown sugar

¼ cup light corn syrup

½ tsp kosher salt

¼ tsp baking soda

½ tsp pure vanilla extract

DIRECTIONS

1. Preheat the oven to 300°F (150°C). Lightly grease a 15 x 10 x 1-inch (38 x 25 x 2.5cm) jelly roll pan. Add the popcorn and pecans to the pan. Mix well and set aside.

2. In a medium saucepan, melt the butter over low heat. Add the brown sugar, corn syrup, and salt; bring to a boil, and boil for 5 minutes without stirring. Remove from the heat and stir in the baking soda and vanilla.

3. Pour the syrup over the popcorn mixture, stirring until the popcorn is evenly coated. Spread into an even layer. Bake for 30 minutes, stirring after 15 minutes.

4. Cool completely and break into pieces. Store in an airtight container on the counter for up to 2 weeks.

MAKE IT AHEAD
You can fully prepare this up to 2 weeks in advance.

TAFFY APPLE SALAD

prep time
20 minutes, plus at least
3 hours to chill

cook time
5 minutes

serves
8

Once a year when the kids were little, I splurged and made homemade taffy apples. The kids loved them! Bill loved them! I loved them! Now that the kids are gone, we enjoy an adult version of that treat—a taffy apple salad we first enjoyed at my sister Louise's home. It's truly a taffy apple without the stick and no caramel stuck between your teeth.

INGREDIENTS

2 cups unpeeled bite-sized apple chunks

1 tsp fresh lemon juice

1 (20 oz/570g) can pineapple chunks

2 cups miniature marshmallows

8 oz (225g) Cool Whip

1 tsp all-purpose flour

½ cup granulated sugar

1 large egg, well beaten

1 (13 oz/350g) can salted redskin Spanish peanuts or cocktail peanuts

DIRECTIONS

1. In a medium bowl, toss the apple chunks with the lemon juice. Drain the pineapples well and reserve the juice. Add the drained pineapple chunks and mini marshmallows to the bowl with the apples. Add the Cool Whip. Gently fold to incorporate. Cover and refrigerate.

2. In a small saucepan, whisk together the reserved pineapple juice, the flour, sugar and the well beaten egg. Cook over medium heat until thickened and the mixture reaches 160°F (71°C). Cover and refrigerate until cool.

3. In a large bowl, combine the chilled fruit and marshmallows, the peanuts, and the chilled sauce. Fold until well combined. Refrigerate for at least 3 hours before serving.

BABS SAYS...
I like to use Cortland, Fuji, Honeycrisp, or Gala apples.

To make your own whipped topping, in a medium bowl, beat 1½ cups heavy cream and 1 tsp pure vanilla extract until stiff peaks form.

MAKE IT AHEAD
This is best eaten the same day, but after it's been well chilled in the refrigerator.

MRS. WILLIAMS'S PEANUT BUTTER BARS

prep time
10 minutes, plus
20 minutes to cool

cook time
none

yield
12

What are your two favorite comfort foods? Mine, too—peanut butter and chocolate! In our family, this became an instant favorite, thanks to Joan Williams who taught at the Growing Tree Nursery School with me so many years ago. After making this for a Halloween party, everyone clamored for the recipe. Think candy meets cookie. It's a 5-ingredient treat that comes together in no time...what are you waiting for?

MAKE IT AHEAD
Prepare these up to
1 day in advance.

INGREDIENTS

1 lb (450g) powdered sugar

2 cups (284g) graham cracker crumbs

1 cup (270g) smooth peanut butter

1 cup (224g) butter, melted

1 (12 oz/340g) bag semisweet chocolate chips, gently melted

DIRECTIONS

1. To a food processor, add the powdered sugar, graham cracker crumbs, and peanut butter. Process until combined.

2. With the motor running, drizzle the melted butter into the mixture until thoroughly combined.

3. Evenly spread the peanut butter mixture in a 10 x 15-inch (25 x 38cm) rimmed baking sheet.

4. Pour the melted chocolate over the peanut butter layer, and spread evenly with an offset spatula.

5. Refrigerate for 10 to 20 minutes, or until cooled. Cut into 2-inch (5cm) squares, and serve. These are best within the first 2 days, but you can store in an airtight container in the refrigerator, layers separated by parchment paper, for up to 5 days, or in the freezer for up to 6 months.

ELLEN'S PUMPKIN LOAF

prep time
20 minutes, plus
6 hours to cool

cook time
1 hour 10 minutes

serves
8–10

I can't count how many different varieties of pumpkin bread I have tried. Some barely had any pumpkin flavor; others were dry and bland. Then, my friend Ellen shared her recipe for the most delicious pumpkin bread that I have ever tasted—a moist bread with a burst of pumpkin in every bite, wrapped in a perfectly proportioned blanket of spices. The chocolate chips are listed as optional—but I have never made this without this "optional" ingredient!

MAKE IT AHEAD
Make this up to 2 days in advance. Store, tightly covered, at room temperature. Make certain it is wrapped at all times, or it will dry out. Store for up to 1 week, tightly covered, in the refrigerator.

INGREDIENTS

1½ cups (192g) all-purpose flour

1 tsp baking soda

½ tsp kosher salt

1 tsp ground cinnamon

½ tsp ground nutmeg

½ tsp ground ginger

½ tsp ground cloves

½ cup (112g) unsalted butter, room temperature

1 cup (200g) granulated sugar

1 tsp pure vanilla extract

2 large eggs, room temperature

¾ cup (170g) pumpkin purée

¾ cup (128g) chocolate chips

½ cup (57g) coarsely chopped walnuts, divided

DIRECTIONS

1. Preheat the oven to 350°F (180°C). Grease the bottom of a 9 x 5 x 3-inch (23 x 12.5 x 7.5cm) loaf pan.

2. Into a medium bowl, sift together the flour, baking soda, salt, and spices.

3. In the bowl of a stand mixer fitted with the paddle attachment, cream the butter on medium-high speed until fluffy.

4. Gradually add the sugar, beating on medium-high speed until light and fluffy.

5. Beat in the vanilla. Add the eggs one at a time, beating well after each addition.

6. With the motor running on low speed, alternate adding the dry ingredients and the pumpkin, beginning and ending with the dry ingredients.

7. Stir in the chocolate chips and ¼ cup (28g) walnuts. Spread in the prepared pan. Sprinkle the top with the remaining ¼ cup (28g) nuts.

8. Bake for 60 to 70 minutes, or until the loaf springs back when touched lightly in the center.

9. Cool for 15 minutes in the pan. Then remove from the pan and cool completely on a wire rack before slicing.

MULLED APPLE CIDER

My neighbor Ann was the authority on all things Williamsburg and colonial. She shared her mulled cider recipe with me one chilly autumn day, and I've been making this every year since. The smooth spices in this liquid apple delight warm the body as well as the soul. Imagine reading a good book next to a crackling fire while sipping on this warm drink.

prep time
20 minutes

cook time
30 minutes

serves
16

INGREDIENTS

1 gal (4 qt/4L) apple cider

7 cinnamon sticks, broken into pieces

2 tsp whole cloves

2 tsp whole allspice

DIRECTIONS

1. In a stockpot, add all of the ingredients. Bring to a boil and simmer, uncovered, for about 30 minutes.

2. Let stand for 15 minutes with the heat off. Strain through a double layer cheesecloth. Chill until ready to serve, and reheat before serving.

BABS SAYS...
Make sure your spices are fresh!

A little whiskey or bourbon may be added to the warm cider on those especially chilly nights.

TRADITIONS TO MAKE YOUR OWN

Open up your home and invite a family who may
be celebrating alone

Go around the dinner table and share
what you are thankful for

Plan an outdoor activity—a game of family flag football
or a turkey trot are our favorites

THANKSGIVING
feast

Thanksgiving is one of my absolute favorite holidays. For years, my mom made the trip from Chicago to be with us. When she was unable to make it, we would get together with neighbors who were also away from family. Over the years, we even made a few trips to New York City to see the famous Macy's Thanksgiving Day Parade. We still joke about the time my Dad brought a step ladder so the kids could get a better view of Santa. One year, we even got together with my daughter's best friend's family who had moved to Connecticut a few short years before from Paris and had never celebrated a Thanksgiving holiday. Thanksgiving truly is without a doubt all about the food and welcoming family and friends to your table.

Typically, we had an early start to the day when Dad and the kids would hit the trail for the high school football game while I made sure everything was set to go on schedule. As the kids got older, the entire family participated in the annual Turkey Trot race.

One of my favorite traditions of the day is sharing gratitude beans. A couple of dried beans are placed on each plate. A small cup is passed around the table. Each person drops one gratitude bean in the cup announcing what they are grateful for. We usually go around two times. These dried beans are then thrown into our turkey soup made from the carcass of the bird the next day. We call it Gratitude Soup.

After lunch, some of us would head outdoors for our fairly competitive family two-hand touch football match while others would take a walk around the neighborhood. Getting fresh air after a big meal is always a wonderful idea. Moving back inside, many were found relaxing and watching football while the little ones entertained the family with their sweet turkey trot dances and talent shows.

As my kids got older, Thanksgiving became more precious than ever. Each year, our table grew with the additions of my daughters-in-law and son-in-law and eight grandchildren. To have all of my children back together under one roof with their own families, even just for a day, becomes more and more priceless with time.

ON THE
TABLE

Cranberry Fluff. 182

Sherried Fruit 183

Green Bean Casserole 185

Spinach & Cheese Bake 187

Grandma Costello's
Buttermilk Biscuits 189

Make-Ahead Turkey Gravy . . .191

No-Peel Make-Ahead
Mashed Potatoes. 193

Sweet Potato Casserole 194

Sweet Potato Balls 195

Country Sausage, Apple &
Herb Stuffing 197

Traditional Roasted Turkey . . .198

Warm Pumpkin Pudding
with Vanilla Ice Cream 201

CRANBERRY FLUFF

This is a fun twist on your average side of cranberries. We make this once a year, and it's over-the-top and around the block. My friend Kim who worked with me for many, many years at the Growing Tree Nursery School shared this family recipe, which soon turned into our family favorite, now an adopted tradition of our own!

prep time
5 minutes, plus overnight to chill

cook time
none

serves
6–8

INGREDIENTS

1 (12 oz/340g) bag of fresh cranberries, washed

1 cup granulated sugar (or less to taste)

1 (20 oz/570g) can crushed pineapple, drained

1 cup mini marshmallows

1 cup heavy cream, whipped

DIRECTIONS

1. In a food processor, finely chop the cranberries, but don't process so much that you have juice.

2. In a large bowl, mix together the cranberries and sugar. Mix in the drained pineapple and mini marshmallows. Fold in the whipped cream. Refrigerate overnight, and serve the next day.

BABS SAYS...
This could be served as a side dish or dessert—it's just that good!

MAKE IT AHEAD
Prepare this up to 5 days in advance.

SHERRIED FRUIT

I love cranberries, but if you're a bit cranberried-out and still want a fruit side on your Thanksgiving table, then sherried fruit may be the answer. This is a combination of several fruits marinating in a buttery sherry sauce overnight and baked the next day. In fact, it's not just for Thanksgiving, but makes a terrific side dish that goes with any beef, pork, or poultry dish. It's not my kids' favorite, but it is my favorite, so it earns a space in my cookbook! A throwback, indeed!

prep time
10 minutes, plus overnight to chill

cook time
35 minutes

serves
8–10 as a side dish

INGREDIENTS

¼ cup unsalted butter

2 tbsp all-purpose flour

½ cup granulated sugar

1 cup sherry

1 (28 oz/800g) can pear halves in natural juice, drained

1 (20 oz/565g) can pineapple chunks in natural juice, drained

1 (14.5 oz/410g) jar spiced apple rings, drained

1 (17 oz/480g) can apricot halves, drained

1 (14 oz/400g) jar maraschino cherries, drained

DIRECTIONS

1. In a small saucepan, melt the butter and flour over low heat, blending until smooth. Slowly stir in the sugar. Add the sherry, stirring constantly until slightly thickened.

2. Combine the sauce and all of the fruit in a 2-quart (2L) casserole dish. Cover and refrigerate overnight.

3. Allow to come to room temperature. When ready to bake, preheat the oven to 350°F (180°C). Bake for 30 minutes, or until hot and bubbling. Serve hot.

BABS SAYS...

I usually use dry sherry, but if you like the extra sweetness, you could use a cream sherry.

It also can be served as a dessert. Imagine vanilla ice cream or pound cake served with this lovely warm, sherried fruit.

MAKE IT AHEAD

This can be baked early in the day and served at room temperature or reheated in a 350°F (180°C) oven for 10 minutes. This gets better over time. It will last for up to 4 days when refrigerated.

GREEN BEAN CASSEROLE

prep time
20 minutes

cook time
50 minutes

serves
12–16

Let's face it, Thanksgiving wouldn't be the same without the traditional green bean casserole. The extra step of making the mushroom cream sauce is worth the effort. The beauty of this dish is also the fact that it can be made a few days before the big event. A shortcut for the fried onion topping is a time-saver that doesn't sacrifice flavor.

INGREDIENTS

2 lb (1kg) green beans, trimmed and cut in half

2 tbsp + 1 tsp kosher salt, divided

¼ cup unsalted butter

1 lb (450g) baby bella mushrooms, stems trimmed, wiped clean, sliced

½ cup thinly sliced onion

3 cloves garlic, minced

½ tsp pepper

Dash of nutmeg

¼ cup all-purpose flour

1½ cups low-sodium chicken broth, heated

1½ cups half-and-half, room temperature

Topping:

1 tbsp salted butter, melted

½ cup seasoned panko bread crumbs

2½ cups canned fried onions (such as Lars Own)

DIRECTIONS

1. Lightly grease a 9 x 13-inch (23 x 33cm) baking dish. Preheat the oven to 375°F (190°C). In a large Dutch oven, bring 4 quarts (4L) water to a boil. Add the green beans and 2 tablespoons salt to the boiling water. Cook for about 6 minutes, or until tender and bright green, being careful not to overcook.

2. While the beans are cooking, fill a large bowl with ice water. Drain the cooked beans in a colander and then immediately plunge into the ice water to stop cooking. Drain again and spread the beans on a baking sheet lined with a double layer of paper towels to dry.

3. In a large skillet, melt the butter over medium heat. Add the sliced mushrooms, onion, garlic, remaining 1 teaspoon salt, pepper, and nutmeg. Cook for 5 to 7 minutes, or until the liquid evaporates, stirring occasionally.

4. Add the flour and combine, and cook for 2 minutes, stirring constantly. Gradually add the chicken broth and half-and-half, stirring constantly. Continue to cook and stir until the sauce is thickened, about 5 minutes.

5. Add the green beans to the mushroom sauce, and stir until the beans are evenly coated. Pour the green bean mixture into the baking dish. Bake for 20 to 25 minutes, or until heated through and bubbling around the edges.

6. While it's cooking, prepare the topping. In a small bowl, combine the melted butter and bread crumbs. Add the onions, and stir to combine. Top the casserole evenly with the topping, and bake for an additional 5 to 10 minutes, or until the onions are golden. If you want the onions crispier, place under the broiler for 30 seconds. Serve hot.

MAKE IT AHEAD

The casserole can be made a few days ahead of serving. Refrigerate the unbaked casserole, covered tightly with plastic wrap, and refrigerate the topping separately. Remove from the refrigerator 1 hour before baking. I don't recommend freezing this.

SPINACH & CHEESE BAKE

prep time
15 minutes

cook time
1 hour

serves
8–10

The first time I had this amazing spinach dish was at my friend Sue's parents' farm in Paris, Illinois. We spent the weekend far from the big city and experienced a peace and tranquility found in few places. After a day of horseback riding (I was petrified) and sitting around a roaring fire, dinner was served. Sue's mom and aunt set a table filled with fresh farm ingredients and savory dishes. This spinach dish was one of them.

MAKE IT AHEAD
Cook this up to 3 days in advance. Reheat, covered, in a 325°F (170°C) oven.

INGREDIENTS

6 large eggs, room temperature

⅓ cup all-purpose flour

½ lb cheddar cheese, hand grated

1 qt (1L) small curd cottage cheese

½ cup unsalted butter, melted

½ tsp salt

Dash of nutmeg

2 (10 oz/285g) bags frozen spinach, thawed and well drained

DIRECTIONS

1. Preheat the oven to 350°F (180°C). Grease a 9 x 13-inch (23 x 33cm) baking dish.

2. In a medium bowl, beat the eggs slightly.

3. In a large bowl, stir together the flour, cheddar, cottage cheese, butter, salt, nutmeg, and spinach. Add the beaten eggs and thoroughly combine.

4. Pour the mixture into the prepared baking dish. Bake for 1 hour, and serve.

GRANDMA COSTELLO'S BUTTERMILK BISCUITS

Imagine eight hungry children (my husband the youngest) gathered around the table anxiously awaiting their food. The older kids were seated nearest the kitchen so they could have first dibs on the passed platters. The biscuits were always served first. My mother-in-law, Hazel, knew how to fill little tummies on a budget. She typically doubled the biscuit recipe! Light, flaky, and delicious—everything you would expect a buttermilk biscuit to be. Just always remember to serve fresh! My granddaughter Grace never had the pleasure of meeting Hazel, her great-grandmother, but she is a huge fan of these biscuits—you could even call them her main food group.

prep time
20 minutes

cook time
20 minutes

yield
18

INGREDIENTS

4 cups (512g) all-purpose flour, plus more to dust

3 tbsp aluminum-free baking powder

2 tsp salt

2 tbsp granulated sugar

1 cup (224g) unsalted butter, cold, cut into small cubes, plus more to grease

2 cups cold buttermilk (plus 3 tbsp, optional, for a buttermilk wash)

DIRECTIONS

1. Preheat the oven to 425°F (220°C). Over a large bowl, using a fine-mesh sieve, sift the flour, baking powder, and salt. Add the sugar, and whisk to combine.

2. Add the cold, cubed butter to the flour mixture. Working quickly, using a pastry blender, combine the butter and flour until pea-sized crumbs are formed.

3. Add the buttermilk, and combine with a fork until the dough comes together. Don't overmix. It should be a loose dough with little flecks of butter throughout.

4. Place the dough on a lightly floured surface. Gently gather the dough until it all comes together. Lightly press or roll the dough to form a 12 x 8-inch (30 x 20cm) rectangle. Fold the right side of the dough toward the center. Fold the left side over the right (like you are folding a giant burrito). Turn the dough one-quarter turn. Repeat the folding and turning twice more. Lightly press or roll the dough until it is about ¾ inch (2cm) thick.

5. Using a 2-inch (5cm) round biscuit cutter, cut circles of the dough, and place almost touching in a large cast-iron skillet prepared with butter.

6. If you'd like to do a buttermilk wash, brush the buttermilk over the tops of the biscuits. Immediately place the skillet in the oven and bake for 18 to 20 minutes before serving.

BABS SAYS...
Follow these very important guidelines, which will change your biscuit-making game forever:

Invest in a biscuit cutter, and when you cut your biscuits, *never* twist the cutter while cutting. This will result in a flat biscuit.

Using a prepared cast-iron skillet gets your biscuits nice and close before baking. It will result in a tall, beautiful biscuit that bakes up instead of out.

You can grate your cold butter right into the flour mixture.

To get the flaky layers we all love, make sure to follow the biscuit-folding technique in step 4.

MAKE-AHEAD TURKEY GRAVY

Thanksgiving should be a day enjoying family and friends and not tied to the stove frantically trying to get everything on the table piping hot. Whatever can be done ahead of time, even weeks ahead of time, is a blessing. The gravy is always the one dish that can really push you over the edge. This is a delicious, easy-to-assemble, make-ahead gravy inspired by Cook's Illustrated that's all ready when you are.

prep time
15 minutes, plus overnight to chill

cook time
4 hours

yield
8 cups

INGREDIENTS

5–7 lb (2.25–3.15kg) turkey wings or thighs

2 medium carrots, cut into 3in (7.5cm) pieces

2 medium celery stalks, cut into 3in (7.5cm) pieces

2 medium onions, quartered

1 head garlic, cut in half

½ cup extra-virgin olive oil

1 tsp salt

½ tsp freshly ground black pepper

2 cups dry white wine

10 cups low-sodium chicken broth

3 bunches fresh thyme

Unsalted butter, if needed

¾ cup all-purpose flour

DIRECTIONS

1. Preheat the oven to 400°F (200°C). To a large, greased roasting pan, add the turkey, carrots, celery, onions, and garlic. Toss with the olive oil, salt, and pepper. Roast, turning occasionally, until the turkey turns deep golden brown, 1 to 1½ hours. Transfer turkey and veggies to a large pot.

2. Place the roasting pan on the stove over 2 burners over medium-high heat. Pour in the white wine. Bring to a boil, and deglaze the bottom of the pan. Turn the heat down and simmer for 5 minutes.

3. Pour the wine mixture into the pot with the turkey and veggies. Add the broth and thyme. Push the turkey down to submerge in the broth. Bring the mixture to a boil over medium heat. Reduce the heat, and gently simmer for 2 hours. With tongs, remove the turkey parts, discarding the skin and bones. Reserve the meat for another use. Pour the broth mixture through a strainer set over a large container, pressing down on the veggies with a spoon to release all the liquid. Discard the vegetables. Refrigerate overnight, or until the fat solidifies on top.

4. When ready to make the gravy, remove the fat and set aside. Heat the stock. Measure the reserved fat, and add additional butter, if needed, to make ¾ cup fat. Melt that fat in a large pot over medium heat. Slowly whisk in the flour to make a roux, whisking until the flour mixture is golden brown and smooth, 5 to 7 minutes. Very gradually whisk in the hot broth, whisking constantly, until the gravy comes to a boil and thickens. Simmer, whisking, until thickened to your liking. Adjust for seasoning. If too thick, just add more stock. If it's lumpy, pass it through a strainer or pop it in a blender. Serve.

BABS SAYS...

It's also a good idea to freeze any leftover stock, which may be used to thin out the gravy, if needed, before serving.

This makes plenty of gravy, so you'll have enough for hot turkey sandwiches and leftovers.

MAKE IT AHEAD

Make this up to 5 days in advance, stored in an airtight container in the refrigerator. Freeze for up to 4 months.

NO-PEEL MAKE-AHEAD MASHED POTATOES

Holidays can be exhausting, and getting food on the table at the right time, hot and ready to go, can be especially challenging. These are my go-to creamy, buttery, lump-free do-ahead mashed potatoes that make entertaining that much more fun and less harried.

INGREDIENTS

5 lb (2.25kg) Yukon Gold potatoes, scrubbed (unpeeled)

¾ cup unsalted butter, melted

1½ cups half-and-half, warmed

2 tsp salt, plus more to taste

½ tsp white pepper, plus more to taste

DIRECTIONS

1. Place the whole potatoes in a large saucepan and cover with 1 inch (2.5cm) of cold water. Bring to a boil over hight heat. Reduce the heat to medium and simmer for about 25 minutes, or until fork-tender.

2. Drain the potatoes and put them back into the now-empty pot. Turn the heat to low and shake the pan with the potatoes to evaporate any excess water.

3. Cut the potatoes in half, and place the hot potato halves into a potato ricer over a large bowl. Press through the ricer. It will naturally peel the potatoes, but you may have to clean the excess peels out from the ricer from time to time.

4. In a small bowl, combine the melted butter, warmed half-and-half, salt, and pepper. Pour 1 cup of the mixture over the riced potatoes, and reserve the rest in the refrigerator. Fold the wet ingredients into the riced potatoes. Cover and refrigerate overnight.

5. About 3 hours before serving, spray the interior of a slow cooker with nonstick spray. Place the potatoes in the slow cooker on low heat. Cover, stirring occasionally, until hot.

6. Reheat the remaining butter and milk mixture, and fold into the mashed potatoes. Taste and season with salt and pepper. Serve.

prep time
15 minutes, plus overnight to chill

cook time
25 minutes, plus 3 hours in slow cooker

serves
8–10

BABS SAYS...
A ricer is a great investment and will guarantee your mashed potatoes are lump-free. OXO Good Grips Adjustable Potato Ricer is my absolute favorite. It peels and rices the potatoes at once.

You don't have to cut the potatoes in half before you rice, but it might be easier.

The golden rule: *never* add anything cold to your mashed potatoes.

MAKE IT AHEAD
Prepare the potatoes up to a day in advance before finishing in the slow cooker.

SWEET POTATO CASEROLE

This is a super simple and delicious sweet potato casserole that calls for baking the sweet potatoes instead of boiling. If you can bake a potato, then you can make this casserole! Everyone who tastes this always asks for the recipe. It will be a sure winner on your Thanksgiving table.

prep time
20 minutes, plus cooling

cook time
1 hour 35 minutes

serves
12

BABS SAYS...
If you have a split crowd, you can always only add marshmallows to one side of your casserole.

INGREDIENTS

6 large sweet potatoes (about 4 lb/2kg), scrubbed

½ cup unsalted butter, melted

2 large eggs, room temperature

¼ cup granulated sugar

1 tsp salt

1 (14 fl oz/400ml) can sweetened condensed milk

1 tsp pure vanilla extract

Topping:

1 cup finely chopped pecans

½ cup firmly packed brown sugar

½ cup all-purpose flour

¼ cup unsalted butter, melted

2 cups mini marshmallows

DIRECTIONS

1. Preheat the oven to 425°F (220°C). Bake the sweet potatoes for 1 hour, or until fork-tender. Once cool, remove the skins.

2. Once the potatoes are cool, preheat the oven to 350°F (180°C). To a stand mixer fitted with the paddle attachment, add the sweet potatoes. Mix until mashed. Add the melted butter, eggs, sugar, salt, condensed milk, and vanilla. Mix until combined. Evenly spread the mixture in a well-greased 9 x 13-inch (23 x 33cm) casserole dish.

3. Prepare the topping. In a medium bowl, combine the pecans, brown sugar, flour, and melted butter. Evenly spread the mixture over the sweet potatoes.

4. Bake for 35 minutes, or until golden brown. Remove from the oven, preheat the broiler, and scatter the marshmallows on top. Broil until just brown, about 5 minutes, watching closely so they don't burn! Serve immediately.

SWEET POTATO BALLS

prep time
25 minutes, plus
6 hours to chill

cook time
1½ hours

serves
12

Here's a twist on the traditional holiday sweet potato casserole, sweet potato balls! This delicious side can be made a day or two ahead before rolling in the honey, butter, and chopped pecan coating. Trust me, you will never miss those marshmallows, but if you do, I've got that covered, too.

MAKE IT AHEAD
Refrigerate the uncooked balls for up to 1 day before baking and serving.

INGREDIENTS

3–4 lbs (1.5–2kg) sweet potatoes

¾ cup firmly packed light brown sugar

4 tbsp unsalted butter, melted

½ tsp ground cinnamon, or more to taste

½ tsp nutmeg, or more to taste

½ tsp salt

½ tsp pure vanilla extract

Coating:

2 tbsp or more unsalted butter, melted

½ cup honey

1½ cups chopped pecans

DIRECTIONS

1. Preheat the oven to 400°F (200°C). Bake the potatoes on a parchment-lined baking sheet until tender, about 1 hour. When soft, peel and mash. Stir in the brown sugar, butter, cinnamon, nutmeg, salt, and vanilla.

2. Cover and refrigerate the mixture for at least 6 hours. When chilled, form into 12 balls and place evenly spaced in a prepared 9 x 13-inch (23 x 33cm) baking dish. They can be covered and refrigerated at this point until ready to bake. When ready to bake, preheat the oven to 350°F (180°C).

3. Make the coating. In a small saucepan, melt the butter and honey over low heat. Roll each ball in the honey butter and then in the chopped pecans. Place back in the baking dish. Bake for 25 to 30 minutes, or until golden. Serve.

COUNTRY SAUSAGE, APPLE & HERB STUFFING

prep time
20 minutes, plus overnight to rest

cook time
1 hour 45 minutes

serves
12

I have been making stuffing for about as long as I can remember. Over the years I'd tweak and alter, but this stuffing is now the one. It truly is the queen of the food parade. Toasting fresh bread cubes really does make a difference.

INGREDIENTS

2 lbs (1kg) hearty white bread, cut into ½in (1.25cm) cubes

¾ cup unsalted butter

1½ cups chopped onions

1½ cups chopped celery

2 Granny Smith apples, chopped

2 tsp kosher salt

1 tsp freshly ground black pepper

2 tbsp fresh thyme leaves or 1½ tsp dried thyme

2 tbsp fresh sage leaves or 1½ tsp ground sage

½ tbsp chopped fresh rosemary or ½ tsp dried rosemary

½ tbsp fresh marjoram or ½ tsp dried marjoram

½ cup chopped fresh parsley leaves

4 cups or more low-sodium chicken or turkey broth, divided

1 lb (450g) sage-flavored breakfast sausage, removed from any casing

3 large eggs, slightly beaten

DIRECTIONS

1. Position the rack in the bottom of the oven and preheat to 250°F (120°C). Spread the bread cubes in a single layer on one or more rimmed baking sheets. Bake for 45 minutes, or until toasted, stirring frequently. Transfer to a very large bowl.

2. In a large skillet, melt the butter over medium-high heat. When the foaming subsides, add the onions, celery, and apples. Season with the salt and pepper. Lower the heat to medium and cook, stirring occasionally, until the vegetables are softened, 5 to 7 minutes. Stir in the thyme, sage, rosemary, marjoram, and parsley, and cook until fragrant, or 1 minute.

3. Add 1 cup broth, and deglaze the pan. Transfer this to the dried bread cubes, and gently combine.

4. In the same skillet, brown the breakfast sausage over medium-high heat, breaking into small pieces with a wooden spoon. Drain the sausage, and add to the bread and vegetable mixture.

5. Add 2 cups broth, or enough to moisten, and gently combine with the bread mixture. Cover and refrigerate until the next day.

6. Remove 1 hour before baking. Position the rack in the bottom of the oven and preheat to 375°F (190°C). Add the eggs and 1 cup or more broth to moisten and combine. Place the stuffing in a greased 9 x 13-inch (23 x 33cm) baking dish, tightly packed. Cover tightly with greased foil. Bake, covered, for 50 to 60 minutes, or until heated through. If you'd like the stuffing browned and toasted, remove the foil covering during the last 10 to 15 minutes of baking. Gently toss the stuffing and then let rest 5 minutes before serving.

BABS SAYS...
I like to bake the stuffing while the turkey is resting.

MAKE IT AHEAD
The bread cubes can be made several days ahead and stored in a resealable bag at room temperature. The rest of the stuffing, up to adding the eggs, can be assembled and refrigerated the day before baking.

Fully cooked stuffing can be frozen and stored in an airtight container and wrapped in foil for 1 to 3 months. Reheat the cooked stuffing in a 350°F (180°C) oven, covered, for 30 minutes, or until warm.

Stuffing can also be frozen immediately before cooking. Place frozen, uncooked stuffing directly into a preheated oven when ready to bake.

TRADITIONAL ROASTED TURKEY

prep time
20 minutes, plus
12–48 hours to brine

cook time
about 4 hours

serves
8–10

I've made wet-brined turkey and no-brine turkey, but this dry-brined turkey is the winner. You do have to plan a few days ahead and have refrigerator space, but it's really just another thing off the list the day of the Big Event. Plus, there's a terrific baking hack I've been using for years that is a great excuse to buy a pizza stone if you don't already own one. The easiest perfect turkey awaits you. Go for it!

INGREDIENTS

6 tbsp coarse kosher salt (such as Diamond Crystal)

2 tbsp baking powder

1½ tsp freshly ground black pepper, divided, plus more to season

12–16 lb (5.5–7.25kg) turkey (or larger), fully thawed, neck and giblets removed

10 sprigs fresh thyme

½ bunch parsley

2–3 small onions, halved, divided

2–3 small apples, halved, divided

6–8 tbsp avocado oil, divided

Nonstick olive oil or avocado oil spray, to coat

DIRECTIONS

1. In a small bowl, combine the salt, baking powder, and ½ teaspoon pepper. Sprinkle—do not rub—the salt mixture evenly over the entire turkey until coated. Place a rack in a large rimmed baking sheet. Place the turkey on the rack. Refrigerate, uncovered, for 12 to 48 hours to dry brine.

2. Remove the turkey from the refrigerator 1 hour before roasting. The baking powder–salt mixture is the key to moist, crispy turkey, so do not rinse it. Just brush off any excess. Season the empty cavity of the turkey with the remaining 1 teaspoon pepper. Add the thyme, parsley, 3 to 4 onion halves, and 3 to 4 apple halves. Season the neck cavity with pepper, and add the remaining onion and apple halves to the cavity. Truss the legs with kitchen twine. Brush the turkey with 4 to 6 tablespoons avocado oil.

3. Place the oven rack in the lowest position. Preheat the oven to 500° F (260°C) with the empty roasting pan on the pizza stone. Cover the turkey breast with a double layer of foil. When the oven is fully preheated, remove the roasting pan from the oven and pour the remaining 2 tablespoons avocado oil into the preheated pan. Place breast-side up in the pan. Lower the oven to 425°F (220°C). Roast the turkey for 45 minutes. Then remove the foil from the turkey breast and spray the breast with olive oil or avocado spray.

4. Lower the temperature to 325°F (170°C). Roast the turkey until the internal temperature of the breast reaches 160°F (71°C) and the legs reach 175°F (79°C). For an unstuffed turkey, it will take about 12 minutes per pound to reach temperature. Let the turkey rest, uncovered, for 45 minutes. Carve and serve with the gravy and dressing.

BABS SAYS...

Make sure to order your fresh turkey a few weeks before Thanksgiving. If using a frozen turkey, make sure to buy it at least a week before to adequately thaw. Thaw in the refrigerator, allowing 1 day per 4 pounds (2kg) of turkey.

This Cook's Illustrated tip is fantastic: place a pizza stone on the lower oven rack, and the roasting pan on top of the stone, allowing them both to preheat. The preheated pizza stone allows the legs to cook at a higher temperature than the rest of the turkey so every part is cooked to perfection.

WARM PUMPKIN PUDDING
WITH VANILLA ICE CREAM

prep time
10 minutes

cook time
40 minutes

serves
8

Trust me on this one...my friend Joanne served this at a family gathering and it has become my new favorite fall dessert. If you're looking for something other than the traditional pumpkin selections, you've found it! It's an unusual baking method, but it works beautifully. With a scoop of vanilla ice cream and a sprinkling of pecans, it's over-the-top and around the block.

INGREDIENTS

1¼ cups (160g) all-purpose flour

2 tsp fresh double-acting baking powder

½ tsp salt

¾ cup (150g) granulated sugar

1 tsp ground cinnamon

¼ tsp ground nutmeg

⅛ tsp ground cloves (optional)

½ cup (114g) pumpkin purée

¼ cup heavy cream

¼ cup (56g) salted butter, melted

1½ tsp pure vanilla extract

Vanilla ice cream, to serve

Topping:

½ cup (100g) granulated sugar

½ cup (107g) firmly packed brown sugar

½ cup (60g) chopped pecans

1½ cups very hot water

DIRECTIONS

1. Preheat the oven to 350°F (180°C). In a medium bowl, whisk together the flour, baking powder, salt, sugar, cinnamon, nutmeg, and cloves (if using). Set aside.

2. In a separate medium bowl, whisk together the pumpkin, cream, butter, and vanilla. Pour the wet ingredients into the dry. Mix to form a thick batter. Pour into a 2-quart (2L) dish.

3. Prepare the topping. In a small bowl, stir together the sugar, brown sugar, and pecans. Spread evenly over the top of the batter.

4. Pour the very hot water over the mixture, and *do not stir*. Place the dish on a baking sheet (it could get messy) and bake for 40 minutes, or until the middle is set.

5. Cool for 5 to 10 minutes before serving. Serve warm with the syrup from baking, vanilla ice cream, and additional pecans.

BABS SAYS...
Make sure you have fresh baking powder.

MAKE IT AHEAD
You could assemble all of the ingredients ahead of time in separate bowls. Just assemble when ready to bake. Also, the batter can be made ahead of time. Just add the topping and the very hot water right before baking.

TRADITIONS TO MAKE YOUR OWN

Hand out sheet music of your favorite Christmas carols,
and sing around the fire or tree

Allow everyone to open one gift before going off to bed
on Christmas Eve—a set of slippers and pajamas to be
worn that night

Visit a local light show or holiday market

CHRISTMAS EVE
festival

Christmas is filled with so many traditions passed on from my parents and my grandparents, Luigi and Vincenza, who came to this country with nothing but their faith and a determination to make a good life in their adopted country. In this land they now called home, many of the traditions from Italy were preserved and passed on.

One of those traditions was the Feast of the Seven Fishes on Christmas Eve. The evening started with shrimp cocktail, baked clams on the half shell, fried and breaded shrimp, and fried smelts. My grandfather's favorites of this annual celebration were the baked eel and baccala (salted cod fish that my grandmother soaked for four days before baking). The different pasta sauces were made with stuffed scungilli, clams, a fish stew, a tuna base, and an anchovy-walnut sauce. Yes, there were plenty of pasta selections. Add to that lobster tails and crab legs, and you get the idea why this was called a feast. The feast of Christmas Eve always ended right before midnight mass, and when we would return home, I can still to this day remember our house always feeling so peaceful and still before the pitter-patter of tiny feet during the Christmas morning rush.

We still like to honor the tradition of the Feast of the Seven Fishes, but we stick to dishes our family and friends will eat! Add to that some truly satisfying homemade treats, and you've created a situation where guests are happy to linger a little longer around the table, enjoying the company and cheer. The menu has changed over the years, but the warmth of the celebration continues. Whether you celebrate Christmas or not, the recipes in this chapter are stellar for any wintertime occasion that's worthy of an exquisite meal.

So much throughout this month is done in anticipation: our Advent calendar and wreath; leaving shoes out on December 6th, for the feast of St. Nicholas; secret Santas; Christmas cards; and a day set aside with the kids and now grandkids to bake our annual Christmas cookies are just some of our family traditions. Did I mention one of my favorites? Christmas movie nights with the movies we watch only during this festive time of the year...my personal all-time favorite *It's a Wonderful Life*, plus my son Bill's favorite *A Christmas Story*, Shawn and Erin's *Christmas Vacation*, and Elizabeth's pick, *The Holiday*. It wouldn't be Christmas at the Costellos without these family traditions to look forward to.

ON THE CHRISTMAS EVE TABLE

Hot Crabmeat Dip 207

Scallop Chowder 209

Gabe's Linguine with
White Clam Sauce 211

Seafood Pasta 212

HOT CRABMEAT DIP

prep time
10 minutes

cook time
10 minutes

serves
a crowd

My husband was hired by a large consumer products company right out of college. We were just a couple of kids new to the corporate scene. Over the holidays, his group was invited to his boss's lovely residence in a suburb of Chicago. We were made to feel right at home and treated to quite a spread of appetizers. This crabmeat dip was served and has since been one of my absolute favorites. It speaks volumes that I still make this dish today—that holiday party sure does seems like a lifetime ago.

INGREDIENTS

3 (8 oz/225g) pkgs cream cheese, room temperature

12 oz (340g) fresh crabmeat

¼ cup dry white wine

¼ cup mayonnaise

2 tsp powdered sugar

2 tsp prepared mustard

2 tsp savory salt

2 tsp onion juice

1 tbsp fresh lemon juice

1 tbsp chopped chives, to garnish

DIRECTIONS

1. Combine all ingredients and heat through in a double boiler, stirring occasionally to prevent it from sticking.

2. Serve in a dish with a variety of crackers on the side.

BABS SAYS...
Onion juice can be found in the aisles of most grocery stores. However, feel free to try freshly grated onion...just be sure to taste it first so it doesn't overpower the dip.

MAKE IT AHEAD
It tastes even better if prepared early! Refrigerate in an airtight container for up to 2 days, and reheat before serving.

SCALLOP CHOWDER

prep time
20 minutes

cook time
25 minutes

serves
8–10

This is a creamy, rich, hearty chowder served as a first course on Christmas Eve. This really is New England in a bowl. It's also enjoyed sitting near a crackling fire on a snowy evening, so you can plan on making this all the winter season.

INGREDIENTS

6 medium russet potatoes, peeled, cut into ½in (1.25cm) pieces

2 small carrots, chopped

2 large celery stalks, chopped

3 cups chicken stock

1 cup clam juice

1 tsp salt

½ tsp freshly ground black pepper

2 bay leaves

1 tsp dry thyme leaves, crumbled

¼ cup unsalted butter, divided

1 lb (450g) white mushrooms, chopped

2 lbs (1kg) dry bay scallops

1 cup dry sherry

2 cups heavy cream

2 egg yolks, lightly beaten

Sweet paprika, to serve

¼ cup chopped fresh flat-leaf parsley

DIRECTIONS

1. To a large Dutch oven, add the potatoes, carrots, and celery. Cover with the chicken stock and clam juice, and bring to a boil. Add the salt, pepper, bay leaves, and thyme. Lower the heat and simmer, covered, until the vegetables are soft.

2. Remove the bay leaves and transfer the soup to a blender, working in batches if needed. Process until smooth, and then return to the Dutch oven.

3. While the vegetables are cooking, in a large skillet, melt 3 tablespoons butter over medium heat. Sauté the mushrooms, and then set them aside on a plate. In the same skillet, melt the remaining 1 tablespoon butter. Dry the scallops and add to the melted butter. Brown for 1 to 2 minutes.

4. Turn up the heat to medium-high, and add the sherry. Reduce this liquid by half (3 to 5 minutes), and remove the skillet from the heat. In a separate medium bowl, whisk together the cream and yolks. Slowly add the mixture into the skillet, stirring constantly. Stir in the mushrooms.

5. Add the cream mixture to the potato base mixture. Heat through and serve in bowls, sprinkled with paprika and parsley.

MAKE IT AHEAD

You can prepare much of this recipe the day before serving. Cook and process the vegetables through step 2 the day before, and store, covered, in the refrigerator. When you are ready to cook the chowder, gently reheat the potato mixture. Proceed with the rest of the recipe.

This chowder will last 3 to 4 days in an airtight container in the refrigerator, but it does not freeze well.

GABE'S LINGUINE
WITH WHITE CLAM SAUCE

My daughter's father-in-law is a great doctor and a great cook. Most importantly, he has one big Staten Island heart. That heart loves Italian food, his specialty being linguine with white clam sauce. This recipe was given to him many years ago from one of his favorite local Italian restaurants. The small Manila clams are very sweet and add to the complexity of this recipe. The addition of shrimp gives it another layer of flavoring not always found in other white clam sauce recipes.

prep time
15–20 minutes

cook time
20 minutes

serves
8–12

INGREDIENTS

2 dozen little neck clams

3 dozen Manila clams

¾–1 cup olive oil

15 cloves garlic (12 cloves sliced into 2 or 3 pieces each, and 3 cloves finely chopped), divided

3 tbsp salted butter

¾ tsp crushed red pepper, or to taste

½ tsp dried oregano

2 bunches fresh flat-leaf parsley, leaves chopped, plus more to garnish

¾ cup white wine, such as Pinot Grigio

4 fl oz (120ml) clam juice

1 lb (450g) large shrimp, cleaned and deveined

2 lb (450g) dry linguine

2 tbsp kosher salt

DIRECTIONS

1. Clean the little neck clams with a brush under cool running water. Refrigerate in a bowl of ice. Clean the Manila clams in the same manner, and keep refrigerated on ice.

2. In a 4-quart (4L) saucepan over low heat, add the oil and the 12 cloves of sliced garlic. Stir. When the oil starts bubbling, add the butter. Raise the heat to medium-low. Stir and sauté the garlic until golden brown, and then remove and discard the garlic pieces.

3. Stir in the crushed red pepper and oregano. Add the 2 cloves chopped garlic, the parsley, white wine, and clam juice to the pot. Stir.

4. Add the little neck clams, and cover the pot. Check and remove the clams as soon as they open up—this will happen quickly. Keep the clams warm, covered in a large bowl. Repeat the process with the Manila clams. Then add the shrimp to the pot, keeping it warm over medium-low heat.

5. In a separate pot, on high heat, boil water for the linguine. Add the salt to the pasta water after it begins to boil. Add the linguine and cook until al dente, or 9 to 10 minutes. Drain the pasta.

6. Toss the cooked linguine in the clam sauce to coat, transfer to a serving bowl, and top with the cooked clams and chopped parsley for garnish. Enjoy.

BABS SAYS...

To *really* flavor the oil, early in the day, marinate the garlic slices in the cold oil in the pot, allowing the garlic to flavor the cold oil before you even add heat. This could be done an hour or two before you start, or while you're prepping the rest of the ingredients. Then follow the recipe as written. This really will add a lovely garlic flavor to your dish.

Cooking the little neck clams and the Manila clams separately ensures that they won't overcook.

SEAFOOD PASTA

prep time
15 minutes

cook time
30 minutes

serves
8

If you're not into Gabe's Linguine with White Clam Sauce (page 211), here is a great red sauce option using lobster, shrimp, and scallops. We save this for Christmas Eve dinner since the addition of the lobster tails and shrimp, along with the scallops, really make it a dish worthy of the holidays or any special occasion. This is your go-to when a delicious, easy, but over-the-top recipe is in the cards.

INGREDIENTS

8 cloves garlic, sliced in thirds

½ cup extra-virgin olive oil, or more as needed

4–8 lobster tails

2–3 lb (1–1.5kg) large shrimp, cleaned and deveined

30–40 bay scallops

2 (35 oz/992g) cans crushed San Marzano tomatoes

2 tsp kosher salt

2 tsp granulated sugar

Crushed red pepper, to taste

½ cup chopped fresh basil or parsley, plus more to garnish

2 lb (1kg) linguine, cooked al dente

DIRECTIONS

1. In a large saucepan, to flavor the oil, sauté the garlic in the olive oil over medium-high heat until golden brown. Discard the garlic.

2. Add the lobster tails and sauté in the oil for 4 to 5 minutes, or until cooked. Remove immediately and set aside to drain.

3. Add more olive oil to the pan if needed. Add the shrimp to the oil, and sauté until pink. Remove the shrimp immediately and set aside to drain.

4. Add more olive oil to the pan if needed. Add the scallops, and cook until opaque. Remove the scallops immediately and set aside to drain.

5. Remove the lobster meat from the shells, and cut into chunks.

6. Add the crushed tomatoes to the now-empty pan. Season with the salt, sugar, and crushed red pepper. Add the basil or parsley, and cook over medium heat for 10 minutes. Add the cooked seafood back to the saucepan and combine. Warm briefly over medium heat until heated through.

7. Pour the seafood sauce over the linguine, and serve immediately. Leftovers are great for up to 3 days. Store in an airtight container in the refrigerator.

BABS SAYS...

The shrimp can be cleaned early in the day since that is the most time-consuming task, or you could buy cleaned and deveined shrimp that are ready to go.

Let the garlic sit in the olive oil for a few hours before starting to cook to really give the oil that garlic flavor. Remember: it's Italian!

ON THE TREATS
TABLE

Peppermint Bark. 216

Chocolate Shortbread Bars . . .217

Chocolate Walnut Fudge 218

Pecan Tassies. 219

Brown-Eyed Susans 221

PEPPERMINT BARK

prep time
5 minutes, plus chilling

cook time
10 minutes

serves
12

If there's one thing that is made only during the holidays and screams Christmas, it's peppermint bark. Why pay a fortune for those sold at specialty shops when you can make your own for a fraction of the price and it's as easy as 1–2–3?

INGREDIENTS	DIRECTIONS
12 oz (340g) good semi-sweet chocolate, chopped 1 tsp peppermint extract, divided 12 oz (340g) good white chocolate, chopped 8 candy canes, crushed	1. Line an 11 x 15-inch (28 x 38cm) baking sheet with parchment paper. In a microwave-safe bowl, microwave the semi-sweet chocolate in 30 second intervals, stirring each time. Don't scorch. When the chocolate has melted, stir in ½ teaspoon peppermint extract. 2. Pour the chocolate mixture onto the prepared baking sheet, and smooth evenly with an offset spatula. Refrigerate for 20 minutes. Meanwhile, melt the white chocolate in the same manner. When melted, stir in ½ tsp peppermint extract. 3. Remove the cooled semi-sweet chocolate from the refrigerator. Spread the melted white chocolate over the cooled layer with the offset spatula. Top immediately with the crushed candy canes and press into the chocolate. Refrigerate for 20 minutes. When cool, cut in squares or break off pieces to serve.

BABS SAYS...
You can't do all your holiday baking in one day! If you store your cookies properly, you can enjoy for weeks. Store only one kind of cookie in each tin. Most should be stored in a cool place. Keep this in mind and you will have a less stressful holiday.

MAKE IT AHEAD
The bark will keep fresh for 2 weeks if stored in an airtight cookie tin in a dark, cool place. It's best not to refrigerate or freeze.

CHOCOLATE SHORTBREAD BARS

This is another family favorite, an easy cookie that pairs a delicate shortbread crust with melted chocolate and toasted nuts. Do I hear heavenly? This was one of mother's tried-and-true Christmas cookies that the family looked forward to during this special time. I now make this with my grandchildren as a tradition.

prep time
15 minutes, plus at least
2 hours to chill

cook time
20 minutes

yield
18

INGREDIENTS

1 cup (224g) unsalted butter, room temperature

1 cup (213g) firmly packed light brown sugar

1 large egg yolk, room temperature

1 tsp pure vanilla extract

2 cups (256g) sifted all-purpose flour

½ tsp salt

2 cups (340g) semi-sweet chocolate chips

1 cup (120g) finely chopped pecans, toasted

DIRECTIONS

1. Preheat the oven to 350°F (180°C). Prepare a 9-inch (23cm) square pan with nonstick cooking spray, and then line with parchment paper.

2. In the bowl of a stand mixer fitted with the paddle attachment, cream the butter and sugar on medium-high speed until smooth and fluffy, 2 to 3 minutes. Beat in the egg yolk and vanilla.

3. In a medium bowl, whisk together the flour and the salt.

4. Add the whisked flour mixture to the creamed butter mixture, and mix until just combined.

5. Press the shortbread evenly into the bottom of the prepared pan. Bake for about 20 minutes, or until golden brown.

6. Immediately upon removing from the oven, sprinkle the chocolate chips all over the crust. Return the shortbread to the oven for 1 minute until the chocolate just starts to soften. Remove from the oven, and with an offset spatula, spread the chocolate into a smooth layer. Sprinkle the toasted nuts over the top.

7. Place the pan on a wire rack to cool completely. Chill for 2 hours or overnight before cutting into 18 bars.

BABS SAYS...
You can use semi-sweet chocolate, milk chocolate, or bittersweet chocolate. You can even use a chocolate bar instead of chips.

If pecans are not for you, use almonds, walnuts, or peanuts. If you'd like to forego the nuts altogether, try using toffee bits.

MAKE IT AHEAD
Store for up to 2 weeks in an airtight cookie tin in a dark, cool place, or freeze for up to 6 months. Let the bars thaw at room temperature and enjoy.

CHOCOLATE WALNUT FUDGE

My daughter Elizabeth and I make this every year to kick off the holiday season. We pick a Friday toward the beginning of December to bake and watch Christmas movies with my grandkids. This is a super easy way to make fudge. Use good-quality chocolate for optimal results.

INGREDIENTS

1 (14 fl oz/396ml) can sweetened condensed milk

¼ tsp ground cinnamon

1 lb (450g) semi-sweet chocolate (such as Ghirardelli), chopped

½ tsp baking soda

Pinch of fine sea salt

¾ cup (85g) coarsely chopped, toasted walnuts (still warm), plus extra ¼ cup (28g) to decorate

DIRECTIONS

1. Grease and line an 8 x 8-inch (20 x 20cm) baking pan with parchment paper, extending the paper over two opposite sides, making it easier to lift the fudge out once it sets.

2. In a medium saucepan, combine the condensed milk and cinnamon. Warm over medium heat, stirring constantly, until the condensed milk is warm and runny.

3. Add the chocolate, baking soda, and salt. Stir constantly for 2 minutes, or until the chocolate is almost melted. Remove the pan from the heat and continue to stir until the chocolate is melted.

4. Working quickly, add the warm walnuts; stir until combined. Spread the mixture into the pan and sprinkle with the extra walnuts. Refrigerate for 3 hours, or until firm. To cut, use a hot, sharp knife. Cut into 1-inch (2.5cm) squares.

prep time
5 minutes, plus 3 hours to chill

cook time
3 minutes

yield
64

MAKE IT AHEAD
The fudge will keep in an airtight cookie tin in a cool, dark place for 2 to 3 weeks, or freeze for 3 months.

PECAN TASSIES

prep time
30 minutes, plus
30 minutes to chill

cook time
20 minutes

yield
48

This is another family favorite Christmas cookie that Mom made every year, but she didn't just make 48 cookies—she would easily make a few hundred of these. These are just two-bite pecan pies with flaky crust and gooey centers.

INGREDIENTS

Dough:

2 cups (256g) sifted all-purpose flour

6 oz (170g) cream cheese, room temperature

1 cup (224g) butter, room temperature

Filling:

3 eggs, room temperature

2 cups (426g) firmly packed light brown sugar

3 tbsp (42g) unsalted butter, melted

2 tsp pure vanilla extract

1½ cups (180g) finely chopped pecans, divided

DIRECTIONS

1. Prepare the dough. In a large bowl, mix the flour, cream cheese, and butter with a pastry blender until a soft dough forms. You could also put all of the ingredients in a food processor and process until a soft dough forms. Wrap in plastic wrap and chill for 30 minutes. Remove the dough from the refrigerator and form 48 balls the size of walnuts.

2. Preheat the oven to 375°F (190°C). In 48 lightly greased mini muffin pan cups (working in batches as needed), place 1 walnut-sized ball into each cup. Press the dough on the bottom and up the sides, forming a small, thin pastry cup.

3. Prepare the filling. In a medium bowl, beat the eggs. Add the brown sugar, butter, and vanilla, mixing very well. Add 1 cup pecans. Divide the filling evenly among the 48 pastry cups. Sprinkle the tops with the remaining pecans. Bake for 17 to 20 minutes, or until lightly browned.

BABS SAYS...
Make sure to lightly spray the pans with a nonstick spray so they will release easily. They could also be dusted with a little powdered sugar.

MAKE IT AHEAD
Keep in an airtight cookie tin at room temperature for up to 2 weeks. Freeze cooled tassies layered between waxed paper in freezer containers. Thaw right in the containers.

BROWN-EYED SUSANS

prep time
10 minutes

cook time
12 minutes

yield
4 dozen

These are one of my all-time favorite cookies that my mom made only at Christmastime. These delicate cookies are light and buttery. The chocolate frosting and the nut topping elevate the simpleness of this tender, easy-to-make holiday treat.

INGREDIENTS

1¼ cups (280g) unsalted butter, softened

3 tbsp granulated sugar

1 tsp almond or vanilla extract

2 cups (256g) all-purpose flour

½ tsp kosher salt

Frosting:

1 cup (115g) sifted powdered sugar

2 tbsp unsweetened cocoa powder

2 tbsp hot water, plus more if needed

½ tsp pure vanilla extract

Whole almond halves, roasted

DIRECTIONS

1. Preheat the oven to 400°F (200°C). Grease a cookie sheet. In the bowl of a stand mixer fitted with the paddle attachment, cream the butter on medium-high speed until light and fluffy. Mix in the sugar, almond extract, flour, and salt until just combined.

2. Roll level tablespoons of dough into small balls. Place on the prepared cookie sheet. Flatten slightly. Bake for 10 to 12 minutes, or until the bottoms are golden brown.

3. Meanwhile, make the frosting. In a medium bowl, combine the sugar and cocoa. Add the hot water and vanilla. Whisk until combined. Add a little more hot water a few drops at a time if needed to thin.

4. Place the baked cookies on a cooling rack. When cool, frost the cookies, and place an almond half in the center of each.

MAKE IT AHEAD
Store cookies in an airtight cookie tin lined with waxed paper. Separate cookie layers with additional waxed paper. These will last for 3 to 4 weeks. These cookies can also be made in advance and frozen.

TRADITIONS TO MAKE YOUR OWN

Make your Christmas day meals ahead of time
so it can be a relaxed day of lounging for all

Pop your breakfast casserole into the oven upon waking

Watch your favorite holiday movie after opening
the presents under the tree

CHRISTMAS DAY
celebrations

Christmas morning always began at the top of the staircase right outside of my kids' bedrooms as they eagerly waited until all were gathered before rushing down to see what Santa had left. For the past 45 years, our traditional Christmas breakfast has been my now famous overnight breakfast casserole and monkey bread, both family favorites my own children have passed on to their children, my grandchildren. While these were baking in the oven, filling our home with the signature aroma of Christmas morning, the kids would be opening the gifts left under the tree. We lounged in our pj's as long as we could, with *The Christmas Story* on repeat.

For many years, Christmas Eve and Christmas Day meant being surrounded by extended family—more cousins, aunts, uncles, and grandparents than you could count. This all changed when we moved away from Chicago. Although the first few years were hard, we eventually found our footing: friends who filled this void. Over forty years ago, we met Joanne and Frank in Virginia, both living away from family like us. We quickly bonded and decided to spend Christmas together. We made it a tradition and alternated houses each year for Christmas dinner. We ended up moving to Ridgefield, Connecticut, and the very next year they followed. All it took was extending an invitation so many years ago, and we've carried on the tradition for decades.

In an Italian family, no matter what the holiday, pasta was always on the menu. The "gravy" was made a few days in advance, and everything was prepped and ready to go. Our entrée for Christmas has been prime rib for many years. It's a special roast fit for such a holiday as Christmas. I introduced Yorkshire pudding to the menu many years ago, and the kids really enjoy this once-a-year treat. Light and creamy tiramisu always hits the spot—a make-ahead must and the perfect ending to an afternoon of eating.

There are a few things you could always count on at our house during Christmas. The kitchen was always the hub of activity, there was always good music like Frankie Valli and the Four Seasons playing in the background, and no matter what, you could always find someone spontaneously breaking out into dancing. Before you knew it, we would end the night with a big dance-off because the Costellos love to dance...and dancing is the ultimate celebration of life!

ON THE
CHRISTMAS DAY
BREAKFAST
TABLE

Overnight Monkey Bread 227

Overnight
Breakfast Casserole.........229

Minnie's Biscotti di Natale....230

Gingerbread Lattes.........230

OVERNIGHT MONKEY BREAD

Your little monkeys, as well as your big ones, will love this addictive overnight breakfast delight. Enjoy this like a monkey would by pulling off pieces of the warm, caramel-coated bread with your hands—no utensils allowed. It's truly, without a doubt, finger lickin' good. I've been serving this to all my monkeys for many years, and it's hands down a family favorite.

prep time
10 minutes, plus
overnight to rise

cook time
35 minutes

serves
8–10

INGREDIENTS

18 frozen unbaked yeast dinner rolls, such as Rhodes (1½ lb/680g)

½ cup chopped raw pecans

½ cup unsalted butter

½ cup firmly packed light brown sugar

1 tbsp ground cinnamon

1 (3 oz/85g) box regular butterscotch pudding mix (not instant)

DIRECTIONS

1. The day before serving, thaw the rolls. Spray a bundt pan with nonstick cooking spray. Spread a small handful of nuts around the pan.

2. In a small bowl, melt the butter. In another small bowl, combine the brown sugar, cinnamon, and pudding mix. Roll the balls in the melted butter, and then roll them in the dry mix. Evenly arrange and layer the rolls in the pan, distributing the pecans throughout. Pour any leftover dry ingredients and butter over top.

3. Cover with plastic wrap and a tea towel, and allow to sit on the counter overnight to rise.

4. In the morning, preheat the oven to 350°F (180°C). Remove the plastic wrap and bake for 30 to 35 minutes. Remove from the pan while still hot. Flip onto a platter and let those monkeys dig in. This will last 2 to 3 days tightly covered and refrigerated, but ours is always devoured long before that.

BABS SAYS...
This can get messy while baking in the oven. It's a good idea to place a foil-lined cookie sheet on the lowest rack of the oven while the bread bakes on the middle rack.

This is meant to be served by pulling a piece from the bread—definitely not cutting. Just ask your monkeys...they know!

OVERNIGHT BREAKFAST CASSEROLE

prep time
10 minutes, plus
overnight to refrigerate

cook time
1 hour

serves
8

After clipping a recipe for an overnight egg casserole from a local newspaper more than 40 years ago, this has become our family's signature Christmas morning breakfast. It has now been enjoyed by three generations of Costellos. The creamy eggs, blanketed in crumbled sausage, with mounds of melted cheese, all nestled in sweet bread send an irresistible aroma wafting through the house, calling everyone downstairs to Christmas morning.

INGREDIENTS

1 lb (450g) breakfast sausage or sweet Italian sausage, removed from any casing

¾ loaf brioche or challah bread or 9 slices any hearty white bread, cut into ½in (1.25cm) cubes

½ lb (225g) grated cheddar cheese (2 cups)

8 large eggs

2½ cups whole milk

1 tsp dry mustard

1 tsp kosher salt

DIRECTIONS

1. The day before serving, grease a 9 x 13-inch (23 x 33cm) casserole dish. In a large skillet over medium heat, brown the sausage, breaking up the meat with a wooden spoon into fine pieces. Drain.

2. To a large bowl, add the meat, bread cubes, and cheese. In a separate medium bowl, beat the eggs. Whisk in the milk, dry mustard, and salt.

3. Pour the egg mixture over the bread cubes, and stir until combined. Transfer the mixture to the prepared casserole dish. Cover with foil and refrigerate overnight.

4. When ready to serve, preheat the oven to 350°F (180°C). Remove the casserole from the refrigerator and uncover. Bake the casserole for 45 to 55 minutes, or until set and bubbly. Allow the casserole to rest for a few minutes before serving. Leftovers are great reheated. Store the fully cooked leftovers in an airtight container for 3 to 5 days in the refrigerator, or freeze for up to 3 months. Just thaw overnight and reheat.

BABS SAYS...
The beauty of this dish is that it's a definite make-ahead casserole, great for a special breakfast or for overnight guests.

You can make this dish your own—get creative! Use breakfast meats of your choice. Cooked bacon and ham are great options. Even mix up the type of cheese.

MINNIE'S BISCOTTI DI NATALE

prep time
15 minutes

cook time
35 minutes

yield
30

There are so many versions of this cookie, but the one served throughout the year in my family was just a plain anise-flavored biscotti. If someone popped over for a cup of coffee (yes, people actually did that years back), you would always have a biscotti to offer with their drink. During the holidays, even the biscotti got a special twist with the addition of candied cherries and pistachios. These are my mom's special holiday version.

INGREDIENTS

3 large eggs, room temperature

½ cup neutral-tasting oil

¾ cup (150g) granulated sugar

2 tsp almond or anise extract

3 cups (384g) all-purpose flour

3 tsp baking powder

½ cup (60g) shelled pistachios

½ cup (57g) dried cranberries

DIRECTIONS

1. Preheat the oven to 350°F (180°C). Line a baking sheet with parchment paper. In the bowl of a stand mixer fitted with the paddle attachment, beat the eggs and oil on medium-high speed until light and foamy. Mix in the sugar and almond extract. In a separate medium bowl, whisk together the flour and baking powder. Add to the egg mixture, and stir to combine. Stir in the pistachios and cranberries.

2. Knead on the counter for 1 minute, adding more flour if the dough is sticky. Divide the dough into 4 portions. Shape into logs 1 to 2 inches (2.5–5cm) thick and 8 inches (20cm) long, pressing down gently on the tops to smooth. Bake on the baking sheet for 20 minutes, or until golden and the center is almost firm.

3. Using a serrated knife, cut each loaf into 1- to 1½-inch- (2.5–3.75cm) thick slices on a slight angle. Transfer the pieces back to the baking sheet in a single layer. Bake for an additional 13 minutes, or until lightly toasted.

4. Remove the cookies and cool on a wire rack. Store in an airtight container at room temperature for up to 1 month. Make sure to line the container with a paper towel to absorb excess moisture, and cover with waxed paper before tightly sealing. These can also be frozen for up to 3 months. When ready to serve, thaw at room temperature.

GINGERBREAD LATTES

Love a fun, themed drink for the Christmas season? If so, you must try my gingerbread latte—a perfect snow day drink to pair with Minnie's Biscotti di Natale.

1 cup 2% or skim milk (lower fat milks develop froth better than whole milk and cream)

2 tbsp molasses or treacle

½ tsp ground ginger

¼ tsp ground cinnamon

1½ cups hot, strong black coffee

1. In a small saucepan, whisk together the milk, molasses, ginger, and cinnamon. Heat over medium-high heat until bubbles form around the side of the pan and the milk is hot.

2. Pour the milk mixture into a small blender (or use a milk frother). Blend until the milk is very frothy.

3. Divide the coffee between 2 or 3 heatproof mugs. Pour in the milk mixture and top with the froth.

ON THE CHRISTMAS DAY LUNCH
TABLE

Mache & Pomegranate
Salad 235

Cranberry-Glazed Brie. 236

Homemade Manicotti 237

Prime Rib of Beef. 239

Yorkshire Pudding 240

Horseradish Sauce 240

Marinara Sauce a.k.a. Gravy. . .241

A True Italian Tiramisu 242

Day-Ahead Eggnog 244

MACHE & POMEGRANATE SALAD

prep time
5 minutes

cook time
none

serves
6

When visiting our daughter at college, we would often shop at a one-of-a-kind local artisanal market called Dorothy Lane. Their deli counter of prepared foods was a half a block long. I signed up for their newsletter, which was mailed to our home in Connecticut. This recipe was featured in a December issue and became our go-to Christmas salad. Mache greens are delicate and tender with a tangy, nutty flavor...the perfect start to your Christmas meal.

INGREDIENTS

4–5 oz (110–140g) mache rosettes greens

½ cup sliced almonds, toasted

1 cup pomegranate seeds

3 oz (85g) goat cheese, crumbled

Dressing:

1 medium shallot, finely chopped

2 tbsp good balsamic vinegar

¼ cup extra-virgin olive oil

Sea salt

Freshly ground black pepper

DIRECTIONS

1. Make the dressing. In a large bowl, whisk together the shallot, vinegar, and oil. Season with salt and pepper to taste.

2. Add the mache greens, almonds, and pomegranate seeds, and toss well. Divide among serving plates and sprinkle goat cheese on each salad. Serve immediately.

BABS SAYS...

You can substitute baby spinach or arugula for the mache greens.

If goat cheese isn't your thing, blue cheese or feta make for a lovely substitution.

I like to buy the pomegranate seeds in prepackaged containers and ready to go, usually found in the produce section during the holiday season.

CRANBERRY-GLAZED BRIE

prep time
10 minutes

cook time
20 minutes

serves
12–16

This festive appetizer oozes rich, buttery cheese in every bite. The cranberry spread topped with the chopped pecans is the crowning touch to this holiday favorite. Make sure to purchase a good quality brie since this soft French cheese is the queen of this dish, taking center stage.

INGREDIENTS

1 (16 oz/450g) wheel of Brie, cold

2 tbsp dark brown sugar

⅓ cup chopped raw pecans

1 tbsp bourbon

½ tsp ground cinnamon

½ tsp ground nutmeg

2 tbsp pure maple syrup

⅔ cup canned whole berry cranberry sauce

1 sprig of fresh rosemary, to garnish

Variety of crackers, toasted baguette slices, apple slices, and pear slices, to serve

DIRECTIONS

1. Preheat the oven to 350°F (180°C). Peel or slice off the top rind of the Brie, being careful not to remove any of the cheese. Place the Brie in a small cast-iron skillet or ovenproof dish.

2. In a small bowl, combine the brown sugar, pecans, bourbon, cinnamon, nutmeg, and maple syrup.

3. Top the brie with the cranberry sauce. Sprinkle with the pecan mixture.

4. Bake for 18 to 20 minutes, or until the cheese is soft and gooey and the fruit is bubbling.

5. Garnish with rosemary. Serve with crackers, or baguette, apple, or pear slices.

BABS SAYS...

Don't be afraid of the brie rind. It's edible and considered a delicacy! Do be sure though to remove any paper wrapping that comes with your brie.

Sprinkle fresh apple or pear slices with a bit of lemon juice to prevent browning.

MAKE IT AHEAD

You can prepare the pecan mixture ahead of time and store in an airtight container in the refrigerator.

HOMEMADE MANICOTTI

prep time
30 minutes

cook time
1 hour

serves
5

This is the easiest homemade pasta you will ever make. The pancakes are tender and delicate, melting in your mouth at the first bite. This makes for a truly impressive entrée. If you're Italian, then it's the *primo piatto* served before the meat course known as the *secondo piatto*. The beauty of this manicotti is that it can be made a few days in advance—or even a month before—and baked when needed. This recipe is easily scaled as desired.

INGREDIENTS

1 batch Marinara Sauce a.k.a. Gravy (page 241)

1 tbsp finely grated Pecorino Romano cheese, to top

Pancakes:

1 cup + 1 tbsp all-purpose flour

½ tsp salt

2 large eggs

1 cup whole milk

Olive oil, to grease

Filling:

½ lb (225g) whole-milk ricotta

1 extra-large egg, slightly beaten

½ cup shredded mozzarella

¼ cup grated Pecorino Romano cheese

2 tbsp chopped fresh flat-leaf parsley

¼ tsp salt

Pinch of freshly ground black pepper

DIRECTIONS

1. Make the pancakes. In the bowl of a stand mixer fitted with the paddle attachment, whisk together the flour and salt. In a small bowl, whisk together the eggs and milk. Add the egg mixture to the dry ingredients, and beat very well on medium-high speed for a minute or more until the batter is thick and totally combined.

2. Brush a 6-inch (15cm) frying pan with olive oil, and heat over low heat. Add 2 tablespoons batter to the center of the pan. Lift the pan from the heat and tilt in all directions to spread the batter to lightly cover the bottom of the skillet. Cook slowly over low heat until set and dry, 30 to 45 seconds. Do not brown, and do not flip—it should resemble a very light crepe. Slide onto a dish. Repeat the procedure, making as many pancakes as the mixture allows. Do not stack the pancakes. This usually makes about 10.

3. Preheat the oven to 350°F (180°C). Coat the bottom a 9 x 13-inch (23 x 33cm) dish with 1 cup marinara sauce. Prepare the filling. In a large bowl, mix together all of the filling ingredients.

4. Place 2 tablespoons filling in a line down the center of each pancake. Fold the two sides over the filling to form an open roll. Arrange the manicotti seam-side down in the dish.

5. Cover lightly with more marinara sauce, and sprinkle with the Pecorino Romano. Cover with foil sprayed lightly with a nonstick spray. Bake for 35 to 45 minutes, or until the manicotti are puffy and the sauce is bubbling. Remove the foil in the last 10 minutes to brown the cheese.

6. Let the manicotti rest for 5 minutes. Spoon more warm sauce on top, and add a sprinkling of Pecorino Romano before serving.

BABS SAYS...

Leave a little gap between each rolled manicotti— they puff up as they bake because of the egg.

MAKE IT AHEAD

Before baking, cover the fully prepped manicotti with plastic wrap and then cover tightly with foil. Refrigerate for up to 3 days or freeze for up to 1 month. When ready to bake frozen manicotti, remove the plastic wrap and replace the foil. Increase baking time to 60 to 75 minutes.

You can also cook the pancakes and freeze them in a freezer bag, each pancake separated by a piece of parchment, until ready to use.

PRIME RIB OF BEEF

The Prime Rib of Beef is to Christmas what the turkey is to Thanksgiving. This is the crown jewel of beef roasts and is fit for a feast like Christmas. The name prime has nothing to do with the grade of meat, but with the place where this roast comes from; it is the primal rib cut between the 6th and 12th ribs. This is one special roast, so if you want to splurge and go for the prime grade, you surely won't be disappointed.

prep time
5 minutes, plus overnight to rest

cook time
2½ hours

serves
10

INGREDIENTS

1 (6–8) lb prime rib roast (or 3-rib standing roast), or larger depending on the number of people

¼ cup olive oil

8 cloves garlic, chopped

2 tsp kosher salt

2 tsp freshly ground black pepper

Horseradish Sauce (page 240), to serve

Yorkshire Pudding (page 240), to serve

DIRECTIONS

1. Ask your butcher to remove the chine (backbone) and connected rib bones, and tie it on the back of the roast. This will make carving so much easier for you.

2. The night before you are serving the beef, make a garlic paste. In a food processor, process the oil, garlic, salt, and pepper. Smear this all over the roast. Return the roast to the refrigerator, uncovered, and let sit overnight.

3. Remove the roast from the refrigerator 3 hours before you begin cooking, allowing it to come to room temperature.

4. Preheat the oven to 525°F (275°C). Place the roast fat-side up on a rack set over a shallow roasting pan. Place in the very hot preheated oven, then lower the oven temperature to 350°F (180°C) as soon as the roast is in the oven.

5. Roast the meat for 16 to 18 minutes per pound, or until it reaches an internal temperature of 120 to 125°F (49–52°C) for medium rare. Make sure to check the internal temperature of the beef at least 30 minutes before you think it is done so you don't overcook it.

6. Remove from the oven and tent the roast with foil. Let it rest for 15 to 20 minutes. The beef will continue to cook and will reach a temperature of 130 to 135°F (54–57°C), medium rare. Serve with the Horseradish Sauce and Yorkshire Pudding.

BABS SAYS...
Invest in a really good meat thermometer. I use one from ThermoWorks.

You can also serve with gravy. Pour off the fat from the pan. Add ¼ cup red wine to the roasting pan and stir up all those browned bits. Add salt to taste and 1 sprig of fresh thyme. Cook on the stove top until gravy boils. Then reduce the heat and simmer for 1 minute. Strain and serve.

YORKSHIRE PUDDING

This light and savory pastry is similar to a popover, a wonderful addition to this Christmas meal. Make Yorkshire pudding once, and it will for sure be a staple on your Christmas table for years to come—we can't imagine prime rib without it.

prep time
10 minutes, plus
1 hour to rest

cook time
25 minutes

yield
6

INGREDIENTS

1 scant cup all-purpose flour

½ tsp salt

½ cup whole milk, room temperature

2 large eggs, room temperature

½ cup water, room temperature

2 tbsp fat drippings or olive oil, room temperature

DIRECTIONS

1. Into a large bowl, sift together the flour and salt. Gradually add the milk, whisking constantly. When smooth, whisk in the eggs, and beat until fluffy and pale yellow. Add the water and beat until the batter bubbles. (You can also beat this batter in a blender.) Let the batter rest for 1 hour.

2. When ready to bake, preheat the oven to 425°F (220°C). Pour 1 teaspoon of fat into each cup of a 6-cup muffin tray. Place in a hot oven for 5 to 10 minutes. Remove the pan with the hot fat drippings. Meanwhile, briefly beat the batter to recombine.

3. Pour the batter into the hot oil, about ¼ to ⅓ cup in each muffin cup. You should hear it sizzle as it hits the hot oil.

4. Quickly return the pan to the oven and do not open the door while it cooks. When the Yorkshire pudding is puffy, golden brown, and crisp, about 20 minutes, it is ready. Remove from the muffin pan and serve.

BABS SAYS...
It's very important to heat the fat so when the batter hits, it sizzles. If you don't hear the sizzle, put it back in the oven and heat more.

Use a heavy-duty metal nonstick pan so the pan won't warp.

MAKE IT AHEAD
You can make the batter the night before. Store covered in the refrigerator. This will even help the batter develop a better flavor. Just be sure to bring to room temperature before baking.

HORSERADISH SAUCE

My son Shawn loves his horseradish sauce, so it is something you can find year after year on our Christmas table. This horseradish sauce is not too spicy, so the whole family will enjoy.

prep time
5 minutes

cook time
none

yield
about 1 cup

INGREDIENTS

¾ cup sour cream

3 tbsp heavy cream

3 tbsp prepared horseradish, or more to taste

DIRECTIONS

1. Combine all of the ingredients and chill. Keep refrigerated until ready to serve.

MAKE IT AHEAD
Make this up to 5 days in advance. Store in an airtight container in the refrigerator.

MARINARA SAUCE
A.K.A GRAVY

Whenever I make gravy, I think of the Italian women before me who left their mark on my heart. Isn't it crazy what food can do? My dear friend and "surrogate mom" Ida was one of those women who had a lasting effect. Ida made her gravy with meat over a two-day period. On the other hand, when under pressure, my mother could whip up a gravy sauce in 20 minutes. Every region in Italy has their own version of this Italian staple. This is a marinara sauce that takes a little longer than 20 minutes, but quicker than 2 days—the best of both!

prep time
10 minutes

cook time
2 hours

yield
1 qt (1L), or enough for 1 lb (450g) pasta

INGREDIENTS

½ cup extra-virgin olive oil

1 large yellow onion, finely chopped

3 large cloves garlic, minced

¼ cup dry white wine

2 (28 oz/800g) cans San Marzano crushed tomatoes

3 tbsp chopped fresh basil

1 small rind Pecorino Romano or Parmesan cheese (optional)

½ tsp kosher salt, or more to taste

¼ tsp freshly ground black pepper, or more to taste

¼ tsp crushed red pepper (optional)

¼ tsp baking soda

DIRECTIONS

1. In a Dutch oven, heat the oil over medium heat until shimmering. Add the onion and sauté for about 5 minutes, or until softened. Stir in the garlic and cook until fragrant, about 30 seconds.

2. Add the wine and tomatoes, increase the heat to medium-high, and let the mixture come to a slow boil.

3. Once boiling, add the basil, cheese rind (if using), salt, pepper, crushed red pepper (if using), and baking soda.

4. Boil for a few minutes, and then adjust the heat to medium-low and simmer for 1 to 1½ hours. Stir the sauce every 10 to 15 minutes, making sure it's not sticking to the bottom of the pan. Rinse one of the empty tomato cans with water, and swirl it around to loosen the excess tomato; transfer the water from can to can to rinse. Add this water sparingly to the sauce if it becomes too thick.

5. Remove the cheese rind (if using), and use the sauce immediately. Store in an airtight container in the refrigerator for up to 1 week, or fully cool and portion into serving-sized freezer bags and freeze for several months.

BABS SAYS...
Always save the rinds from your grated cheese. Pop them in the freezer until ready to use in your pasta sauce. These really add such a rich depth of flavor to your sauce.

Make this in a slow cooker. Prepare the base through step 2. Add this mixture and the rest of the ingredients to the slow cooker. Cook on low for 6 to 8 hours. You can drape a dish towel over the slow cooker and then place on the lid. The towel will help absorb excess moisture

Don't leave sauce out at room temperature for more than 2 hours because bacteria can start to form.

MAKE IT AHEAD
Prepare this up to 1 week in advance, stored in an airtight container in the refrigerator, or freeze in freezer-safe bags for up to 6 months.

A TRUE ITALIAN TIRAMISU

prep time
25 minutes, plus
6–24 hours to rest

cook time
none

serves
12 or more

This is a family recipe I've tweaked throughout the years, and if I do say so myself, it's the absolute best dessert after a holiday meal. In Italian, *tiramisu* actually means "pick me up," and after one taste of this elegant, creamy, light (and did I say easy?) dessert, you will realize how desperately you needed this pick me up. In fact, no matter what time of day it is, it's always tiramisu time!

INGREDIENTS

1 cup fresh-brewed espresso or very strong coffee, cooled

½ cup coffee liqueur, such as Kahlúa

6 large pasteurized eggs, room temperature, separated

⅔ cup (133g) granulated sugar

¼ tsp salt

1½ lb (680g) mascarpone (kept cold)

1 (17.6 oz/500g) pkg ladyfingers

4 tbsp good-quality Dutch-processed cocoa powder

Grated semi-sweet chocolate (optional), to top

DIRECTIONS

1. In a wide, shallow bowl or dish, combine the espresso and coffee liqueur, and set aside.

2. In the bowl of a stand mixer fitted with the whisk attachment, beat the egg yolks, sugar, and salt on high speed until the sugar is dissolved and the mixture is light and creamy, 3 to 4 minutes.

3. Add the mascarpone and beat on medium speed until smooth, 30 to 45 seconds, being careful not to overprocess and deflate the yolks. Carefully transfer the mixture to a large bowl.

4. Thoroughly clean and dry the stand mixer bowl. Beat the egg whites until soft peaks form, 2 to 3 minutes. Using a rubber spatula, gently fold the whites into the mascarpone mixture until no white streaks remain, being very careful not to deflate.

5. Roll the ladyfingers in the espresso mixture for no more than a second each. Place the dipped ladyfingers in a 9 x 13-inch (23 x 33cm) casserole dish, breaking the ladyfingers as needed to fit neatly into the dish and cover the bottom in an even layer. They should be tightly fitted.

6. Spread half of the mascarpone mixture over the layer of ladyfingers, using a rubber spatula to spread to the sides and into the corners. Place 2 tablespoons of the cocoa powder in a fine mesh strainer and dust the cocoa over the mascarpone.

7. Add another layer of the espresso dipped ladyfingers, and spread the remaining mascarpone gently on top. Finish by sprinkling with the remaining 2 tablespoons cocoa powder.

8. Cover with plastic wrap and refrigerate for 6 hours to 1 day. Before serving, sprinkle with additional cocoa and chocolate shavings (if desired).

BABS SAYS...

The beauty of this delicious dessert is that it has to be made in advance, which is such a blessing during the hectic holiday season.

Tiramisu is always spooned, never cut, so get your spoon out when ready to serve.

You can easily cut this recipe in half.

Make sure to use pasteurized eggs.

DAY-AHEAD EGGNOG

prep time
5 minutes, plus
6–24 hours to chill

cook time
12 minutes

serves
4

Once a year, I treat myself to this quintessential holiday beverage, eggnog. Its smooth, creamy, whipped taste is a wonderful standalone treat. If you love your homemade eggnog during this festive season and don't have a lot of time, this is your recipe. The hardest part is waiting to enjoy!

INGREDIENTS

6 large pasteurized egg yolks

⅓ cup granulated sugar

2 cups half-and-half

1 cup heavy whipping cream

½ tsp ground nutmeg, plus extra to sprinkle

¼ tsp ground cinnamon (optional)

¼ tsp pure vanilla extract

1½ tsp brandy or rum or flavoring (optional)

DIRECTIONS

1. In a medium bowl, whisk the yolks and sugar until the sugar dissolves.

2. In a medium saucepan, heat the half-and-half and heavy cream over medium-high heat until bubbles appear around the side of the pan. Gradually whisk the hot cream into the egg mixture a little at a time to temper the eggs, whisking constantly. Then pour the mixture back into the same pan.

3. Add the nutmeg and cinnamon. Stir constantly on medium-low heat until the temperature reaches 160°F (71°C) on a candy thermometer, and the mixture thickens and coats the back of a spoon. Remove from the heat. If desired, strain through a fine-mesh sieve. Stir in the brandy (if using).

4. Pour the mixture into a heatproof jar with a resealable lid. Chill for 6 hours or overnight until cold. When ready to serve, shake vigorously, and pour into serving glasses. Sprinkle individual servings with extra nutmeg, and serve.

BABS SAYS...

If you would like to add alcohol to your eggnog, start with ¼ cup brandy, bourbon, rum, or whiskey, added along with the vanilla, or after cooling the eggnog. Add more to taste, if desired.

Make sure to use pasteurized eggs.

MAKE IT AHEAD

You can make this up to 4 days in advance. Refrigerate in an airtight jar. Shake vigorously before serving.

INDEX

A

Apricot Bourbon–Glazed
Ham, 86–87
Aunt Chickie's Famous
Ribs, 136–137

B

Baked Caramel Corn,
168–169
Baked Reuben Casserole,
78–79
beans, Hilda's Ranch Baked
Beans, 134–135
beef
Grilled Stuffed Flank
Steak, 138–139
Oven-Barbecued
Brisket, 30–31
Prime Rib of Beef,
238–239
Whiskey-Glazed
Corned Beef with
Cabbage, 72–73
beverages
Bloody Marys, 34–35
Day-Ahead Eggnog,
244–245
Elaine's Champagne
Punch, 96–97
Elderflower Mimosas,
112–113
Gingerbread Lattes,
230–231
Irish Coffee, 76–77
Mulled Apple Cider,
176–177
Prosecco with
Strawberry Purée,
64–65
Southern Slushies,
144–145
birthday cakes, 114–123
Ford's Perfect Chocolate
Cake, 118
menu, 117
Pancake Breakfast,
122–123
Rainbow Sprinkle
Funfetti Cake, 119
Smash Cake, 121

Bloody Marys, 34–35
Bobby's Court Buffalo
Wings, 42–43
Brats & All the Trimmings,
152–153
breads
Cheater's Pecan
Cinnamon Rolls,
108–109
Corn Pudding, 166–167
Ellen's Pumpkin Loaf,
174–175
Grandma Costello's
Buttermilk Biscuits,
188–189
Grandma's Easter Bread,
92–93
Irish Soda Bread, 70–71
Minnie's Biscotti di
Natale, 230–231
Overnight Monkey
Bread, 226–227
Soft Pretzels, 155
Yorkshire Pudding, 240
breakfast and brunch
French Toast Overnight
Casserole, 104–105
Overnight Breakfast
Casserole, 228–229
Pancake Breakfast,
122–123
Perfect Egg Brunch
Casserole, 106–107
Broccoli Salad, 128–129
Brown-Eyed Susans,
220–221
brunch. See breakfast and
brunch

C

cakes. See desserts and
sweets
casseroles
Baked Reuben
Casserole, 78–79
Country Sausage, Apple
& Herb Stuffing,
196–197
French Toast Overnight
Casserole, 104–105

Green Bean Casserole,
184–185
Overnight Breakfast
Casserole, 228–229
Perfect Egg Brunch
Casserole, 106–107
Spinach & Cheese Bake,
186–187
Cheater's Pecan Cinnamon
Rolls, 108–109
cheese
Cheddar Pecan
Cheeseball, 24–25
Cranberry-Glazed Brie,
236
Creamy Beer Cheese
Dip, 150–151
Hot Corn Dip, 40–41
Spinach & Cheese Bake,
186–187
chili. See soups and stews
Chocolate Shortbread Bars,
217
Chocolate Walnut Fudge,
218
Christmas Day, 222–247
Cranberry-Glazed Brie,
236
Day-Ahead Eggnog,
244–245
Gingerbread Lattes,
230–231
Homemade Manicotti,
237
Horseradish Sauce, 240
Mache & Pomegranate
Salad, 234–235
Marinara Sauce a.k.a.
Gravy, 241
menu, 225, 233
Minnie's Biscotti di
Natale, 230–231
Overnight Breakfast
Casserole, 228–229
Overnight Monkey
Bread, 226–227
Prime Rib of Beef,
238–239
A True Italian Tiramisu,
242–243
Yorkshire Pudding, 240
Christmas Eve, 202–221
Brown-Eyed Susans,
220–221

Chocolate Shortbread
Bars, 217
Chocolate Walnut
Fudge, 218
Gabe's Linguine with
White Clam Sauce,
210–211
Hot Crabmeat Dip,
206–207
menu, 205
Pecan Tassies, 219
Peppermint Bark, 216
Scallop Chowder,
208–209
Seafood Pasta, 212–213
Corn Pudding, 166–167
Corn Salad, 132–133
Country Sausage, Apple &
Herb Stuffing, 196–197
Cranberry Fluff, 182
Cranberry-Glazed Brie, 236
Creamy Beer Cheese Dip,
150–151

D

Day-Ahead Eggnog,
244–245
desserts and sweets. See also
birthday cakes
Baked Caramel Corn,
168–169
Brown-Eyed Susans,
220–221
Chocolate Shortbread
Bars, 217
Chocolate Walnut
Fudge, 218
Corn Pudding, 166–167
Fresh Peach Pie,
142–143
Grandma Soden's
German Cheesecake,
158–159
Irish Beer Cupcakes,
74–75
Italian Cream Cake,
110–111
Minnie's Biscotti di
Natale, 230–231
Mom's Four-Layer
Delight, 32–33

Mrs. Williams's Peanut Butter Bars, 172–173
Pecan Tassies, 219
Peppermint Bark, 216
Pots de Crème, 62–63
Texas Sheet Cake, 48–49
Traditional Carrot Cake, 94–95
A True Italian Tiramisu, 242–243
Warm Pumpkin Pudding with Vanilla Ice Cream, 200–201
dips
  Creamy Beer Cheese Dip, 150–151
  Hot Corn Dip, 40–41
  Hot Crabmeat Dip, 206–207

E

Easter, 80–97
  Apricot Bourbon–Glazed Ham, 86–87
  Eileen's Strawberry Salad, 84–85
  Elaine's Champagne Punch, 96–97
  Elma's Curried Rice, 90–91
  Grandma's Easter Bread, 92–93
  menu, 83
  Roasted Leg of Lamb, 88–89
  Traditional Carrot Cake, 94–95
Eileen's Strawberry Salad, 84–85
Elaine's Champagne Punch, 96–97
Elderflower Mimosas, 112–113
Ellen's Pumpkin Loaf, 174–175
Elma's Curried Rice, 90–91
entertaining, point of, 14

F

family involvement, 13
food prep, 15
Ford's Perfect Chocolate Cake, 118

French Toast Overnight Casserole, 104–105
fruit
  Fresh Peach Pie, 142–143
  Sherried Fruit, 183
  Summer Fruit Salad for a Crowd, 130–131
  Taffy Apple Salad, 170–171

G

Gabe's Linguine with White Clam Sauce, 210–211
German Roasted Potato Salad, 156–157
Gingerbread Lattes, 230–231
Good Luck Salad, 26–27
Grandma Costello's Buttermilk Biscuits, 188–189
Grandma's Easter Bread, 92–93
Grandma Soden's German Cheesecake, 158–159
Greek Salad with Aunt Louise's Dressing, 54–55
Green Bean Casserole, 184–185
Grilled Stuffed Flank Steak, 138–139
guest list, 14

H-I-J-K

Halloween, 160–177
  Baked Caramel Corn, 168–169
  Corn Pudding, 166–167
  Ellen's Pumpkin Loaf, 174–175
  menu, 163
  Mrs. Williams's Peanut Butter Bars, 172–173
  Mulled Apple Cider, 176–177
  New Pond Farm Chili, 164–165
  Taffy Apple Salad, 170–171
ham, Apricot Bourbon–Glazed Ham, 86–87
Hilda's Ranch Baked Beans, 134–135

Homemade Manicotti, 237
Horseradish Sauce, 240
Hot Corn Dip, 40–41
Hot Crabmeat Dip, 206–207

Irish Beer Cupcakes, 74–75
Irish Coffee, 76–77
Irish Soda Bread, 70–71
Italian Cream Cake, 110-111

L

lamb
  Marinated Lamb Chops, 60–61
  Roasted Leg of Lamb, 88–89
Lebanese Pilaf, 56–57
Lemon-Barbecued Chicken, 140–141

M

Mache & Pomegranate Salad, 234–235
No-Peel Make-Ahead Mashed Potatoes, 192–193
Make-Ahead Turkey Gravy, 190–191
Marinara Sauce a.k.a. Gravy, 241
Marinated Lamb Chops, 60–61
menu planning, 15
menus
  birthday cakes, 117
    Ford's Perfect Chocolate Cake, 118
    Pancake Breakfast, 122–123
    Rainbow Sprinkle Funfetti Cake, 119
    Smash Cake, 121
  Christmas Day, 225, 233
    Cranberry-Glazed Brie, 236
    Day-Ahead Eggnog, 244–245
    Gingerbread Lattes, 230–231
    Homemade Manicotti, 237

Horseradish Sauce, 240
Mache & Pomegranate Salad, 234–235
Marinara Sauce a.k.a. Gravy, 241
Minnie's Biscotti di Natale, 230–231
Overnight Breakfast Casserole, 228–229
Overnight Monkey Bread, 226–227
Prime Rib of Beef, 238–239
A True Italian Tiramisu, 242–243
Yorkshire Pudding, 240
Christmas Eve, 205, 215
  Brown-Eyed Susans, 220–221
  Chocolate Shortbread Bars, 217
  Chocolate Walnut Fudge, 218
  Gabe's Linguine with White Clam Sauce, 210–211
  Hot Crabmeat Dip, 206–207
  Pecan Tassies, 219
  Peppermint Bark, 216
  Scallop Chowder, 208–209
  Seafood Pasta, 212–213
Easter, 83
  Apricot Bourbon–Glazed Ham, 86–87
  Eileen's Strawberry Salad, 84–85
  Elaine's Champagne Punch, 96–97
  Elma's Curried Rice, 90–91
  Grandma's Easter Bread, 92–93
  Roasted Leg of Lamb, 88–89
  Traditional Carrot Cake, 94–95
Halloween, 163
  Baked Caramel Corn, 168–169

Corn Pudding,
166–167
Ellen's Pumpkin
Loaf, 174–175
Mrs. Williams's
Peanut Butter
Bars, 172–173
Mulled Apple Cider,
176–177
New Pond Farm
Chili, 164–165
Taffy Apple Salad,
170–171
Mother's Day, 101
Cheater's Pecan
Cinnamon Rolls,
108–109
Elderflower
Mimosas, 112–113
French Toast
Overnight
Casserole, 104–105
Italian Cream Cake,
110–111
Mixed Greens Salad,
102–103
Perfect Egg Brunch
Casserole, 106–107
New Year's Day, 23
Bloody Marys, 34–35
Cheddar Pecan
Cheeseball, 24–25
Good Luck Salad,
26–27
Mom's Four-Layer
Delight, 32–33
Oven-Barbecued
Brisket, 30–31
Virginia au Gratin
Potatoes, 28–29
Oktoberfest, 149
Brats & All the
Trimmings,
152–153
Creamy Beer Cheese
Dip, 150–151
German Roasted
Potato Salad,
156–157
Grandma Soden's
German
Cheesecake,
158–159
Pickled Carrots &
Daikon, 154
Soft Pretzels, 155
Sriracha Aioli, 154
St. Patrick's Day, 69
Baked Reuben
Casserole, 78–79

Irish Beer Cupcakes,
74–75
Irish Coffee, 76–77
Irish Soda Bread,
70–71
Whiskey-Glazed
Corned Beef with
Cabbage, 72–73
summer barbecue, 127
Aunt Chickie's
Famous Ribs,
136–137
Broccoli Salad,
128–129
Corn Salad, 132–133
Fresh Peach Pie,
142–143
Grilled Stuffed
Flank Steak,
138–139
Hilda's Ranch Baked
Beans, 134–135
Lemon-Barbecued
Chicken, 140–141
Southern Slushies,
144–145
Summer Fruit Salad
for a Crowd,
130–131
Super Bowl, 39
Bobby's Court
Buffalo Wings,
42–43
Hot Corn Dip,
40–41
Sausage Bisquick
Bites, 46–47
Slow-Cooked Pulled
Pork Sandwiches,
44–45
Texas Sheet Cake,
48–49
Thanksgiving, 181
Country Sausage,
Apple & Herb
Stuffing, 196–197
Cranberry Fluff, 182
Grandma Costello's
Buttermilk
Biscuits, 188–189
Green Bean
Casserole, 184–185
Make-Ahead Turkey
Gravy, 190–191
No-Peel Make-
Ahead Mashed
Potatoes, 192–193
Sherried Fruit, 183
Spinach & Cheese
Bake, 186–187

Sweet Potato Balls,
195
Sweet Potato
Casserole, 194
Traditional Roasted
Turkey, 198–199
Warm Pumpkin
Pudding with
Vanilla Ice Cream,
200–201
Valentine's Day, 53
Greek Salad with
Aunt Louise's
Dressing, 54–55
Lebanese Pilaf,
56–57
Marinated Lamb
Chops, 60–61
Pots de Crème,
62–63
Prosecco with
Strawberry Purée,
64–65
Slow-Cooked
French Onion
Soup, 58–59
Minnie's Biscotti di Natale,
230–231
Mixed Greens Salad,
102–103
Mom's Four-Layer Delight,
32–33
Mother's Day, 98–113
Cheater's Pecan
Cinnamon Rolls,
108–109
Elderflower Mimosas,
112–113
French Toast Overnight
Casserole, 104–105
Italian Cream Cake,
110–111
menu, 101
Mixed Greens Salad,
102–103
Perfect Egg Brunch
Casserole, 106–107
Mrs. Williams's Peanut
Butter Bars, 172–173
Mulled Apple Cider,
176–177

N

New Pond Farm Chili,
164–165
New Year's Day, 20–35

Bloody Marys, 34–35
Cheddar Pecan
Cheeseball, 24–25
Good Luck Salad, 26–27
menu, 23
Mom's Four-Layer
Delight, 32–33
Oven-Barbecued
Brisket, 30–31
Virginia au Gratin
Potatoes, 28–29
No-Peel Make-Ahead
Mashed Potatoes,
192–193

O

Oktoberfest, 146–159
Brats & All the
Trimmings, 152–153
Creamy Beer Cheese
Dip, 150–151
German Roasted Potato
Salad, 156–157
Grandma Soden's
German Cheesecake,
158–159
menu, 149
Pickled Carrots &
Daikon, 154
Soft Pretzels, 155
Sriracha Aioli, 154
Oven-Barbecued Brisket,
30–31
Overnight Breakfast
Casserole, 228–229
Overnight Monkey Bread,
226–227

P-Q-R

Pancake Breakfast, 122–123
party day, 17–18
appetizers, 17
atmosphere, 17
beverages, 17
traditions &
entertainment, 18
party space, 14
pasta
Gabe's Linguine with
White Clam Sauce,
210–211
Homemade Manicotti,
237
Seafood Pasta, 212–213

Pecan Tassies, 219
Peppermint Bark, 216
Perfect Egg Brunch
    Casserole, 106–107
Pickled Carrots & Daikon,
    154
pork
    Aunt Chickie's Famous
        Ribs, 136–137
    Brats & All the
        Trimmings, 152–153
    Sausage Bisquick Bites,
        46–47
    Slow-Cooked Pulled
        Pork Sandwiches,
        44–45
potatoes
    German Roasted Potato
        Salad, 156–157
    No-Peel Make-Ahead
        Mashed Potatoes,
        192–193
    Sweet Potato Balls, 195
    Sweet Potato Casserole,
        194
    Virginia au Gratin
        Potatoes, 28–29
Pots de Crème, 62–63
poultry
    Bobby's Court Buffalo
        Wings, 42–43
    Lemon-Barbecued
        Chicken, 140–141
    Traditional Roasted
        Turkey, 198–199
Prime Rib of Beef, 238–239
Prosecco with Strawberry
    Purée, 64–65

Rainbow Sprinkle Funfetti
    Cake, 119
reasons to celebrate, 13
rice
    Elma's Curried Rice,
        90–91
    Lebanese Pilaf, 56–57
Roasted Leg of Lamb,
    88–89

S

salads
    Broccoli Salad, 128–129
    Corn Salad, 132–133
    Eileen's Strawberry
        Salad, 84–85

German Roasted Potato
    Salad, 156–157
Good Luck Salad, 26–27
Greek Salad with Aunt
    Louise's Dressing,
    54–55
Mache & Pomegranate
    Salad, 234–235
Mixed Greens Salad,
    102–103
Summer Fruit Salad for
    a Crowd, 130–131
Taffy Apple Salad,
    170–171
sandwiches, Slow-Cooked
    Pulled Pork Sandwiches,
    44–45
sauces
    Gabe's Linguine with
        White Clam Sauce,
        210–211
    Horseradish Sauce, 240
    Make-Ahead Turkey
        Gravy, 190–191
    Marinara Sauce a.k.a.
        Gravy, 241
    Sriracha Aioli, 154
Sausage Bisquick Bites,
    46–47
Scallop Chowder, 208–209
Seafood Pasta, 212–213
Sherried Fruit, 183
Slow-Cooked French
    Onion Soup, 58–59
Slow-Cooked Pulled Pork
    Sandwiches, 44–45
Smash Cake, 121
Soft Pretzels, 155
soups and stews
    New Pond Farm Chili,
        164–165
    Scallop Chowder,
        208–209
    Slow-Cooked French
        Onion Soup, 58–59
Southern Slushies, 144–145
Spinach & Cheese Bake,
    186–187
Sriracha Aioli, 154
St. Patrick's Day, 66–79
    Baked Reuben
        Casserole, 78–79
    Irish Beer Cupcakes,
        74–75
    Irish Coffee, 76–77
    Irish Soda Bread, 70–71
    menu, 69

Whiskey-Glazed
    Corned Beef with
    Cabbage, 72–73
summer barbecue, 124–145
    Aunt Chickie's Famous
        Ribs, 136–137
    Broccoli Salad, 128–129
    Corn Salad, 132–133
    Fresh Peach Pie,
        142–143
    Grilled Stuffed Flank
        Steak, 138–139
    Hilda's Ranch Baked
        Beans, 134–135
    Lemon-Barbecued
        Chicken, 140–141
    menu, 127
    Southern Slushies,
        144–145
    Summer Fruit Salad for
        a Crowd, 130–131
Super Bowl, 36–49
    Bobby's Court Buffalo
        Wings, 42–43
    Hot Corn Dip, 40–41
    menu, 39
    Sausage Bisquick Bites,
        46–47
    Slow-Cooked Pulled
        Pork Sandwiches,
        44–45
    Texas Sheet Cake, 48–49
Sweet Potato Balls, 195
Sweet Potato Casserole, 194
sweets. See desserts and
    sweets

T-U-V

table setting, 14
Taffy Apple Salad, 170–171
Texas Sheet Cake, 48–49
Thanksgiving, 178–201
    Country Sausage, Apple
        & Herb Stuffing,
        196–197
    Cranberry Fluff, 182
    Grandma Costello's
        Buttermilk Biscuits,
        188–189
    Green Bean Casserole,
        184–185
    Make-Ahead Turkey
        Gravy, 190–191
    menu, 181

No-Peel Make-Ahead
    Mashed Potatoes,
    192–193
Sherried Fruit, 183
Spinach & Cheese Bake,
    186–187
Sweet Potato Balls, 195
Sweet Potato Casserole,
    194
Traditional Roasted
    Turkey, 198–199
Warm Pumpkin
    Pudding with Vanilla
    Ice Cream, 200–201
timing of food, 15
Traditional Carrot Cake,
    94–95
Traditional Roasted Turkey,
    198–199
A True Italian Tiramisu,
    242–243

Valentine's Day, 50–65
    Greek Salad with Aunt
        Louise's Dressing,
        54–55
    Lebanese Pilaf, 56–57
    Marinated Lamb Chops,
        60–61
    menu, 53
    Pots de Crème, 62–63
    Prosecco with
        Strawberry Purée,
        64–65
    Slow-Cooked French
        Onion Soup, 58–59
Vanilla Buttercream
    Frosting, 120
vegetables
    Broccoli Salad, 128–129
    Corn Salad, 132–133
    Green Bean Casserole,
        184–185
    Spinach & Cheese Bake,
        186–187
Virginia au Gratin Potatoes,
    28–29

W-X-Y-Z

Warm Pumpkin Pudding
    with Vanilla Ice Cream,
    200–201
Whiskey-Glazed Corned
    Beef with Cabbage, 72–73

Yorkshire Pudding, 240

DECADES OF FAMILY TRADITIONS

My grandparents, with whom so many traditions began, and their 22 grandchildren

Our Wedding Day 1970: Featuring **Elaine's Champagne Punch**

Make this on page 97

1973: Four generations of women in my family—my grandmother Vincenza, my mother Minnie, my sister Louise, myself, and my niece Lisa, Westchester, Illinois

Shawn's Baptism 1978: My son's baptism, after which **Mom's Four-Layer Delight** was served, La Grange Park, Illinois

Find this on page 33

1969: Grandma Costello from **Grandma Costello's Buttermilk Biscuits (page 189),** Chicago

Find her delicious Easter bread on page 93

New Year's Eve 1955: Grandma Vincenza (of **Grandma's Easter Bread**), Chicago

Make Aunt Louise's salad dressing (page 55)!

Valentine's Day with my grandkids Charlie, Ford, and Scooter

Valentine's Day 1963: My sister Louise (of **Greek Salad with Aunt Louise's Dressing**), Chicago

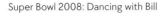

Super Bowl 2008: Dancing with Bill

St. Patrick's Day 2017: Enjoying Guinness in Dublin, Ireland

Easter Morning 1986

Easter: Cooking with my grandkids Grace, Charlotte, and Finley

Mother's Day 1986

Mother's Day 1981: Brunch at Joanne Casey's home, Virginia

Mother's Day 1962: Brunch with my aunts and mother, Chicago

Mother's Day 2008: And also celebrating Mom's 90th birthday, Chicago

Elizabeth's Birthday 1990: My daughter's 5th birthday, Growing Tree Nursery School

Erin's Birthday 1983: My daughter's 2nd birthday, Richmond, Virgina

Shawn's Birthday 1980: My son's 3rd birthday, Richmond, Virginia

Bill's Birthday 1977: Celebrating my son's birthday with my mom Minnie, Chicago

Fourth of July 1983: Uncle Al's famous birthday barbecue, Oakbrook, Illinois

Summer Barbecue 1981: Virginia

Oktoberfest

Halloween 1983: My daughter wearing my hand-sewn pumpkin costume, Ridgefield, Connecticut

Halloween 2006: My granddaughter Grace and I, The Growing Tree Nursery School

Halloween 1990: My daughter in the same costume

Halloween: Charlie in the same costume

Thanksgiving 1950: Grandma Vincenza in the kitchen

Christmas Eve 1950: My mom Minnie (of **Minnie's Biscotti di Natale, page 230,** and other Christmas treats); my father, Jimmie; with me in tow, Chicago

Christmas Morning 1986: Ridgefield, Connecticut

Minnie's Biscotti di Natale (page 230)!

Christmas Day 1977: Aunt Chickie (of **Aunt Chickie's Famous Ribs**), Westchester, Illinois

Find them on page 137

With all eight of my beautiful grandkids

Season's Greetings

Christmas 1953: Marshall Fields, Chicago

AUTHOR'S ACKNOWLEDGMENTS

I could never have completed this labor of love without the complete support and encouragement of my husband, Bill. To say he's been there every step of the way is an understatement. Also, to my treasures, my children: Bill, Shawn, Erin, and Elizabeth. To my daughters-in-law, Jen and Jennifer, and my son-in-law Ray. And to my eight amazing grandchildren: Mary, Grace, Matthew, Charlotte, Finley, Charlie, Ford, and Scooter, who bring such joy and sheer wonder to my life and give me so many reasons to celebrate!!

A special thank you to my youngest child, Elizabeth, who played a large part in this unexpected journey of *Brunch with Babs*, who saw something in me that I didn't see in myself. As a retired preschool teacher of 25 years, I never thought there was a second part to my story.

One afternoon a few years back while sitting in her kitchen, she casually mentioned, "Hey, Mom, you should try TikTok,"...and the rest is history.

PUBLISHER'S THANKS

Proofreaders Polly Zetterberg, Lisa Himes, Lisa Starnes
Indexer Celia McCoy

Food Photography:
Art Director Rebecca Batchelor
Photographer Daniel Showalter
Chef Ashley Brooks
Food Stylist Lovoni Walker

Lifestyle Photography:
Art Director Kathleen Jerry
Photographer Rikki Snyder
Creative Brand Director Alexandra Thompson
Food Stylist Ashley Holt
Makeup Stylist Alexandria Gilleo
Hair Stylist Desiree Leigh
Wardrobe Stylist Inge Fonteyne
Assistant to the Art Director Lauren Perlman
Shoot Assistant Laura LaFond Patterson

Tabletop propping for photography:
Juliska
Carolina Irving and Daughters
Staub
Amanda Lindroth
Adirondack Store

Wardrobe for photography:
Talbots

ABOUT THE AUTHOR

Barbara Costello, warmly known as Babs to followers of *Brunch with Babs*, is a home cook, mother of four, grandmother of eight, and the adopted grandmother to millions of viewers. She shares time-tested and delicious party favorites on TikTok and Instagram.